# Lyrics for the BRIDE of GOD

Also by Nathaniel Tarn

Old Savage/Young City, 1964

Selection: Penguin Modern Poets No. 7, 1965

Where Babylon Ends, 1968

The Beautiful Contradictions, 1969

October, 1969

The Silence, 1969

A Nowhere for Vallejo, 1971

Section: The Artemision, 1973

The Persephones, 1974

The Heights of Macchu Picchu (Pablo Neruda), 1966

Con Cuba, 1969

Stelae (Victor Segalen), 1969

Selected Poems (Pablo Neruda), 1970

# Lyrics for the BRIDE of GOD

## Nathaniel Tarn

A NEW DIRECTIONS BOOK

ACKNOWLEDGMENTS
Grateful acknowledgment is made to the editors and publishers of books and magazines in which some of the material in this volume first appeared: *All You Can Eat, Chicago Review, Clear Creek, Earth-Ship, Fervent Valley, Fuse, Io, The Lampeter Muse, Los, Mojo Navigator, Raster, Red Crow, Salamander, Seizure, Sixpack, Sumac: Active Anthology, Tree, TriQuarterly, Truck, Unmuzzled Ox.*

The whole of "Section: The Artemision" was brought out in 1973 as *Lyrics for the Bride of God, Section: The Artemision* by Christopher's Press for Tree Books (David Meltzer, editor), Santa Barbara, California.

The passages from Kate Millet's *The Prostitution Papers* (Copyright © 1971 by Basic Books; Copyright © 1973 by Kate Millet) are reprinted by permission of the author and her agent, Georges Borchardt, Inc., 145 East 52nd Street, New York 10022.

Manufactured in the United States of America
First published clothbound and as New Directions Paperbook 391 in 1975
Published simultaneously in Canada by McClelland & Stewart, Ltd.

Library of Congress Cataloging in Publication Data

Tarn, Nathaniel.
    Lyrics for the Bride of God.

    (A New Directions Book)
    I. Title.
PR6070.A57L9        821'.9'14        74–23354
ISBN 0–8112–0565–7
ISBN 0–8112–0566–5 pbk.

New Directions Books are published for James Laughlin
by New Directions Publishing Corporation,
333 Sixth Avenue, New York 10014

For N. and P. R. T.

# CONTENTS

# Lyrics for the BRIDE of GOD

# A PREFACE IN THE FORM OF AN ARRIVAL

*The poems you are about to hear belong to the time of wandering.*

*I wandered among killers and victims until I had murdered the throng
and died at my own hands.*

*There may be no more murders and no more suicides. I no longer wander.*

*Something has happened. Someone has arrived. I am not alone.*

*The arrival may best be spoken of as a she. Perhaps. I may call her
the Friend.*

*She is what I thought of as my own presence. The heart's is her weight.*

*If I am silent in her company, my solitude is still as bird noise.*

*There is no possible loneliness in her company.*

*If another comes, she comes not in her place, but comes free.
And if I go to another, I do not give the Friend up to her, but go free.*

*With her, nothing is imposed on another, nor can anyone impose on me.*

*Given love, I can accept it in her name, at its own just weight.*

*Not given love, we abide, she and I, in our own place.*

## II

*There seemed to be a great gap between others and herself. Pure illusion!*

*In the scales of justice, she is the true discussion of all weight.*

*The making of great calm is her throne beside me.*

*Talk to her as if she were the Friend of now, though she be forever: in
that way, there can be no loss.*

*She clothes the bachelor and leaves the husband bare.*

The three secrets:

*1) If I were to walk with her along the street, I would become visible.*

*2) If she could take me in her mouth, I would speak.*

*3) With strength, the tower of gentleness will not arise. With gentleness, the tower of strength will arise.*

IV

*You, now, whatever your name is, (insert name),*
*I leave her with you, I lend her to you for a while—*
*or will borrow you back from time after a while, it is all one.*

*I leave your image together with hers, asleep in the city,*
*you assume your name gradually, you become what you have always been.*
*Though asleep in your arms, she remains steady.*

*All night your hands have been making containers for my sleep*
*and my dreams have glazed them.*
*Our hands glazed into the clay with hers, and the fire is lit.*

*You are everywhere this morning in the trees around me.*
*Head cocked, I watch the trees / I may just hear you.*
*The birds are everywhere, they jump, you make no movement.*
*I will borrow her back from you whenever you need your freedom.*

## SECTION: THE KITCHEN (1): THE NEED FOR WRITERS

They said we don't know about a female aspect of God
it goes against the grain and has little to do with the tradition
our fathers rammed down our throats with castor oil
    but I was very much in love with her and could have eaten her shit
had she ever asked, but she never did in that time.

It was in several other countries and she often died in her prime.

> She was supposed to collect my particle of soul
> came by on that last visit to take it out of me by force
> because I wasn't ready to let go of it at any price
> and she recited the good authors, talked about Grete and Bea:
> how even the top performers had been reconciled in the end—

and who was I to object for the good of Israel /
                                I mean: we had *that* sort of pride?

### II

> —I'll stay alone from now on
> won't collect any other soul until I have yours
> that stage of my life is over and you can have my chastity too
> since that's what you've been wanting in the first place
>                it's all so simple
> although you have a genius for complications sure enough

>   (but I had wanted it some time before that
>   and perhaps no longer wanted it now.)

### III

I said I'd feel small without the particle  mean  and diminished
                     poor  poor  poor  poor  poor
sort of two-dimensional and unable to excite anybody
and lost without the light of my life quite put out
with no energy to go on to anything new or finish anything begun

                            (reference: the Orphic myths)

  and also and more importantly I'd never be able to write again—

but she said how this was going to be a different world
                    without need of writers
          because everything would be perfect from now on
          we'd spend the whole time looking into her eyes
                    as she looked into her husband's
Jesus I said how dull but it was the wrong thing to say
          she was going on about a house she would build me
                    I could travel to and from


                    she was whispering all the time
          don't kill us  don't kill us  don't kill us

I suppose she meant the holy particles which united her and me
I felt guilty because I had led her to believe that we might make it
          and now she was going back without my particle
                    and would have nothing to do
          with her life except raise those children
                    she did not want and had never loved
          so how could one cry vengeance and say yes
                    one had yes fallen out of salvation /

she said it's all there for you whenever you want it
                    you are everything still.


## SECTION: THE KITCHEN (2): OF SEDUCTIONS THE FIRST AND ONLY


                    Periphery of vision,
                    at blade of breath and tongue,
          at tip of thought — the very tendrils of the possible:
          at the:  I hardly dare, I think not, it can't  be done:
                    kumari of the spirit
                    untainted virgin of a calculation
                    in the glow of never-known. . .

          To go towards joy in this case being sure to inflict some pain
          and to have been so often at the genesis of pain in others!
                    The unbearable hovers at the edge of my eyelids:
                    fields I have fertilized and left to rot,
                    dead birds in their hundreds uneaten,
          bees choking of their own gold in the gathering Fall —
                    NO: WE CANNOT DO THIS AGAIN?

but / the excitement in your voice
    the getting away together sketched on the mind
        skating like Winter at bay,
            the stutter in your voice down the phone
as we come up for air to breathe within ourselves —
    you: scattered from thought to thought with lightspeed
caressingly over my surge of thought, and perhaps
    caressingly over my surge of body
            because I know wanting you
        I know wanting you, kumari of the spirit
            as yet unborn!


## WHILE


all over the world tidal waves sweep thousands born
    thousands unborn on the shores of hunger
and while THIS is beginning, kumari of the touch of birds!

            In mental Indies friendship spreads
like the white ink of a secret over the city we breathe
    the messages of an instantaneous future call out to us, singing,


        at the very frontier of the word
        we need to speak, to begin starting,
        to begin beginning in our hands,
        to start starting in our feet towards us,
        kumari of the breast pointing to earth
        and the yoni pointing to heaven:


finger of crime, scatting its touch on my hands and lips,
    with the light insults to language you love,
            the silken *fucks* and *shits*,
            to the point of beginnings —


## DAMN WOMANIZERS YES


but: don't I want it, don't you want it, don't we want it, in the dark,
            HERE IN THE DARK HERE,
here in the dark, in the tidal wave of ocean, in the only crime?

## SECTION: THE KITCHEN (3): CURRICULUM VITAE

I don't budge from this kitchen.
It's the only furnished part of a vast house
        with tables and chairs apart from the usual appliances
and a recipe book from a forgotten country.

I once saw that it was dark beyond the kitchen
in the basement and on the three floors
in all the various rooms smelling of carpet-cleaner and wall-wash.
I've been told it goes on being dark there by the visitors.

   She doesn't live in this kitchen which is a solitary place
   I know that on some nights
      she sits in the living room beyond darkness
   with her own choice of books
          and sometimes plays with her cosmetics in another
   and there are other nights
      she sleeps in the nude upstairs face down on the pillows
                        waiting for a surprise attack.

### II

She has not yet made up her mind (or perhaps this is projection)
   whether or not to come into   and occupy the house
   she is empowered   that is to say she has the means
   to bring light into the house and turn on all the appliances

   which would flush me from the kitchen where I live
as I've said to friends and students: like something out of Beckett

            perhaps she is afraid of the bills!

### III

        Pieces of her occupy certain windowledges
I see her hands from time to time in the fireplace
        her crotch and creases play havoc with the mirrors
and I eat the fruit of that tree as the cannibals did in Atlantis

            *O ekeine periple!*

the victim's body smoked and carved / upside down beside the door!

Eating and making love
in Eden:
EVOE VIRGINIA!
one total complex.

## IV

The art, perhaps, IS to forget
white clouds   smoke in interstices
mist on the synapses linking thought to thought.
You will be killed my son: no one can last this way
but can you swear it matters?

Pocahontas in the city
Bagdad on Hudson
belly-dance girl
dry-run on 42nd street:

There was ambition
desire in coming here / a goal in sight
to write
the inches of Atlantis down before she drowned

(and to take on that journey some sort of homely Helen
not gone to whore in Troy, no —
stayed at home, and dull become a little
until that wreck of Asia gone through the middle island reached at last
these Western stuccoes). . .

But there'd been nothing in Atlantis
to stitch thought to thought about her
no coherence:   the center had *not* held
and the circumference had gone crazy
even among the ones with kindly dispositions.

You will not get it out of my mind
that my ways are not your ways he'd said before
and this is an Israeli girl
and our frontiers won't give an inch.

## V

After the age of revolutions/
after the age of actions/
into the age of talk merely.

7

So that what I do if she wants me on that trip
is accept her one day, refuse her the next, she is exasperated
into loving me far more extremely than she has ever loved
and cooking for me all day in the kitchen
                    by special dispensation
and washing all my shirts
and hanging herself up at nights to be had all ways.
And I explain that I cannot explain
                    that I'm not responsible
                        that we *dichtern*
have never been solid citizens at the best of times since Plato
are male chauvinist sexist pigs
                    (vide Arendt on Dark Times and B(é)B(é).

The chronology of that golden age escapes me
            exactly when she ceased burning like a furnace upon me
and joy turned aside and forced me to hide
                    which is also to say:

        between loving her and not loving her and forgetting her
        there is some cultural as well as personal smoke
                        and my tragedy
                        or ours
                    is that of the time

                        and the time is also of Atlantis.


## SECTION: THE KITCHEN (4): THE SECOND SEDUCTION, ITS SHADOW


You do not come, do not call, do not fetch, do not propose,
kumari, lady of all beginnings,
rap of hard rain on leaves, hard slap of waters,
clatter to water of noise, rattle of torrents,
fall of child-rivers and father-mother-rivers,
                        into, surrounded by vassals,
        the princessing, the ever-queenly sea!

Only — at open doors — at my light step,
up your stairs, stairs of the brownstone, or skyscraper,
or whatever it is you inhabit I have the address of,
in night of city, with light step, assaulting all those flights

into the open runway of your smile, the five o'clock shuttle,
straddled with legs apart while your sex
                              points at the roof and calls—

                    calls with a bleeding month
                    with a whole load of papoose
            in potential, for the fertilization: seed, root, leaf,
        with all that blood, the horns of the dilemma of our days!

                    It is said in the Book of Splendor
        in the book of splendor that Moses going up the mountain fucked
                    that he fucked the Bride of God
            between her teeth and she produced the holy word
                which he took down against the calves and idols
            and thereafter was unable to do anything on earth again
                        to his human wife:

                        BENE,  ALORA

You tell me of the old loves, dismembered and eaten,
cannibalized with a look of horror on your face, and vacancy,
grin bloody with their foam of sins, their tails
gripped between your teeth and snapped, kumari of the sharp vagina,
                virgin of saw, serrated tongue and tooth,
                bearing me back to the first loss

        that immemorial loss in the jungles of childhood,
                        the little / little toys
                the bows and arrows taken from me that were
                so small the smile of my brother in the night
                        bleeding with memories
                could never hide them between dusk and dawn,

mounting your stairs, coming to the grip of your body,
my hands between your thighs, between your breasts,
between your buttocks in the forcing of
                              fruit in the darkness
pips and stones spurting out
resounding on the ground with a thunder-noise, a tidal wave,

and my deep cry, moan of stag, moan of hound, or bear,
baying cry that seduces your own cry from your lips, that have not

called, come, fetched, proposed, collected or enwrapped,
recycled like old pulp, old timber on the flood of the wave,

far up the silent coast of pines, and rocks, and shipwrecked dreams. . .


## SECTION: THE KITCHEN (5): THE COLLECTION


Prognostications visions omens dreams
desires transformed into a telegram
it is time for her to come and collect her elected
she perishes of boredom in her own home
        and would devote some time to the home of the elected

which she'll paint, clean-out, spring-clean, fall-clean,
season-break
        until a temperate sun shines always in at the windows.

  And her eyes will not remember
      the crimes committed against her
         will not contain reproaches
           will not
              number the sins by the rings around the iris
  will not enumerate the trees of paradise.

II

She'll take a hand of me for her purposes
and the other for his perhaps
and a leg of me for her walks along the ridges
and the other for his visitation to the hells
one side for the laying out of cities
the other for land-use and the fields
and in greater detail:
        the eye for seeing but of course
        and the nose for smell
        ears:hearing / mouth:taste
and the mind for the repartition of all things in their right places.

Of the other details we'll make
first a child in the mystery of her own belly
and the life which the child is to live for a long time
        and then attribute the power of surprising

to the ordinary, unadorned, untalented human body
so that a pair of eyes no very different from any other
will seem to one beholder like the very openings onto heaven
    I mean: we must enrich this world.


    Though she come to take her own again
  is it not with the creation of the universe we are concerned
she and I in our                       unfathomable love!

### III

    Parting the night like a forest
    with that gesture of teaching
    more beautiful than Justice
we'll make of the way she came a broad swath cut through the forest
    and lie down inside it on the very divide.
    Autumn will smell of Spring
    decay of birth   blood of the snow
    what there is in me to answer to my own,
    ambitions rise from death
                I have been wrapped in:


    and she will be a tree in my heart
      her roots pinning me down to this existence!

### IV

Whether I see or not
          (according to the fancy of the wind
          the lateness of the heat
          the season's no to dying)
   all those great birds in line along the sky
               sprung from her branches
          their shadow haunts the mind
          like wooden hawks above a chicken coop
              and flesh or not
          great burst of wings or not
          far kettles swirling with a thousand birds
          invisible to all but angels now or not
yet I *have* seen them


      and those wing-tips collecting me
        scooping my eyes from their sockets


      the flight midday perhaps if I can find the time. . .

And you have launched the word, now,
                    the word, now, in your heart,
enraptured on cone of wind into spiraling sky,
when drunk on the lips of your spirit,
                    kumari of the smile,
I go beyond all beginnings to silence and repose. . .


                    I say that my interpretation
is of a pair with other interpretations
                    and that my version of the tale
does not conflict with other versions
                    and that my imagination is of a purity
which encompasses other imaginations
and that this is the way you have wanted it from the beginning,
                    o ivory goddess!


### HERMENEUTICS:

because they shall spend a thousand years on the talmud of your name
and the ins and outs of your form from the body of stillness
and a thousand thousand on the commentaries of your life
and the involutions and evolutions of your spirit, o as yet unwritten!

                    In the tidiness of your days
                    where you have laid up a space for me,
                        *scriptor ludens* with a vengeance,
                    food-bringer, crosser of mountains,
                    perpetually made earth, that am come —
                    body of sky in its perfections, to go
                    into your cloud, into, into


### THE UNWRITTEN BLUE
### THE UNFORMULATED BLUE OF YOUR PERFECT SEDUCTION
### AND / END / OF / THOUGHT!

### II

You lie on your own length, perfected in stillness,
and moving only to bring me unrequiting into your stillness,
    for here there is no motion of love,

though love circles round itself in silence,
here there is no oscillation of male into female,
no syrup of longing from yoni to lingam,
                              but only thought meeting,
and what they call mind-fucking in certain circles,
                              wd. they knew what they intended!
It was a long time ago in my thought,
it was once upon a time in my longing,
this meeting of our inner selves, this turn
of eye to eye, and inner eye to inner eye,
                              and ear to ear,
and hand to hand along the wires of knowledge,
                              thick with spittle,
  thick with the grease of desire. . .

### III

                  They have come here to die
            those I have killed and those killed in my name,
            thin as shadows of sheets of paper on the wind,
      and the call to human progress in a world unfit for creatures.
                  They have come here to die
                        fish, birds & beasts,
      from the borders of the forest that are in flames now, beloved,
        o kumari of vegetation, goddess of thin lip and smile
                  while everything returns into our arms!

                        I go in quiet
                  in the white wind of cities with no name,
            and I bear your name almost forgotten, almost unspoken,
                        under my tongue
                  into the silence of this never ending crime.


## SECTION: THE KITCHEN (7): THE NEWS


I have been against the generating of children from the beginning
because of the stupidity into which they are born
            because of the war
because they are themselves a cause of war
because they rob us of our freedom
because they are cretins in their long infancy
            and try our patience beyond all bounds:

for private and public reasons both I was against them
        and can now add: pollution.

                        Yet when I read the news —
I having told her
            very suddenly
that among
    those things I wished to do to her, with her, on her,
            was the fathering
            (and she had mentioned the matter in our youth,
            I mean the youth of our love)
    of a child
                IN THE VERY PREVIOUS LETTER
she then saying in the very next it might interest you to know
                I thought I was carrying
            until today my god
your child
and (READ all thoughts in stanza 1 plus valid thoughts of her own)
                yet had decided to keep it,
        to live with a little of you:

                                    but
    I was wrong:   it dissolved in a flood of blood —
            I dipped to a chair head in hands.

                        II

                    As she lost that blood
                    to lie drained and white
                    did she cry too and lose eye-water
                    drip mucus from her nose and snot
                    bleed from anywhere else
                    try to bleed from anywhere else
                    shit rather liquid
                    was there urine also mixed with the blood
                    was anyone crying or losing waters
                    anywhere near her?
                        She was always reticent about such things.

                        III

Of those animals that eat their young
why do they do it, and does it give them any pleasure
gastronomic or otherwise?
                population pressure?
                    jealousy?
                            desire for solitude?

14

I'd drink that blood if I could
/if she'd kept it
to return the strength into myself
to keep it for another try
lying together
shooting her everywhere I want to
directing specifically
into her sweet doors
that never smell except of work
and what I think of as rosefood
more of that blood
towards the building of another child.

### IV

And you could come for me then Woman of God with your basket
scythe   knife   rake
whatever it is you take us in with
you could come to me then, with that blood in my mouth
and collect all that Israel in one sweep

before I'd shot that goy cunt
I'd been forbidden all the days of my life
Sweet Lord keeping your gentile to yourself!

you could get me then
in that one moment
ending history not a second too soon,

WERE YOU TO LEAVE ME THOUGH   in that sweet, oiled salvo
it would begin again the story of the Jews and gentiles
and another world cycle would have to be suffered.

### V

Cry for my son / my daughter any color,
mourn complexions I shall never kiss:
of me   birch with a silver shadow,
of her   darker than Lebanon

while she builds up again
the blood of work and leisure

and if you don't want me now, if I'm not required this moment

bring me into her valleys again, for my peace.

## SECTION: THE KITCHEN (8): THE ARCHEOLOGY OF THE SEDUCTION

You say you have thought of me so often in so many ways and I say
I have thought of you so often in so many ways and you say
the simplest way of going about this complex business is to ask
how things are with you
    and I make all the noises about everything being o.k.

And I find you are going to be in town tonight but I won't see you,
your feet are going to be on the same ground as mine
I've always thought
    the most poignant thing that can happen to lovers is
to have their feet on the same earth and not be seen together

BUT WHEN:    INCIPIT / INCIPIT

*Sweet flower Variety:* Variety opens, and fields of wheat lie down,
fields of barley lie down as under a tidal from the sea,
or heaven blows in such a rage as none has seen since Isaiah or Job,
the berries fall from the trees among "hunters & gatherers,"
the fish bites his way right through the net,
the birds rise out of traps in a slow motion ghost-dance,
the worlds of eaten and eater change place with each other
    and the great cities lie down in a mist of ruin.

I go down to our beginnings, kumari pulcherrima, in all the languages
I go back to where we hung from the same paps and fingered toys,
where we played in pens together and lay out on couches in the sun
exploring our nether worlds and marveling at their secrets,

I go back to the day I said marry me, my hands under the faucet,
    as one had washed his hands on a previous occasion,
    and to the day we ate in a dingy place
after I'd lectured on what was and what wasn't conducive to salvation —

and we'd decided that Variety flower was the sweetest that blows.

II

How long exactly
do you think it took those first parents of ours
after they had eaten
that apple and lain down among the ruins,

with all the future of this earth already crushed about them
— or so the orthodox like to think (that *felix culpa*!) —
how long exactly do you think
it took them to get through and to begin to wonder
what it is made their flesh creep as if
    they'd read the book about them


. . . . . . . . . . . . . . . . . . . . .


and tenderness to set in after love?


## SECTION: THE KITCHEN (9): THE IMPERFECTION


Among rods   among pistons
    in the noise of the senseless machines
  her unintelligent servants
      who tried to please me with hypotheses
        approximations of pleasure:
I held out for
slid out of her for

each drop of seed expended in true ritual
    each time and every time mind you
      having to be
   per-  FECT,

        and swore
      not to accept
  a substitute.

And she said:
    Imperfect as is thy servant Lord
    unendowed with the means to please
    crippled from birth by many accidents
    crushed by insensitive men into frigidity
    brought up like an American before
    the sexual revolution
how CAN I do more than
    to be open at all times like a shop
for whatever coin you will expend
    looking after your own consumption?

we winked at each other
in the blood bath          and admitted
    "we are good at taking on each other's sins."

## II

She swam inside me
    exploring Egypt in my feet
        the Promised Land in my head
she met Eve inside me and gave a sign of recognition
then she told me that my geography was confused
and that I didn't know the path from Egypt to Israel

      She took my hands
      and placed them on the shores of the Red Sea
      and said now swim

      The next morning she fell down several times
      and said she was unable to pass water.

## III

And if  at the time of going
if  at the time of handing in receipts
my goods, my deeds, transactions, chattels, servants, dogs,
I have to get together and take along with me into her lassitude,
and if  at the time of traveling
I go without knowledge of the purpose of going
picking up my fragments in this town or that
strewn along some country lane on this continent or that
    or in that stranger's eyes
      my hardly knowing I had left them there. . .

      Will she be picking up after me
      following me about
      saying you've left this sock on the sill
      and why can't you put away your shirts
      like everyone else?

the way a woman suffers. . .

## SECTION: THE KITCHEN (10): THE INNER SEDUCTION

The night has gone by,
along the shore of our faces,
the night of anonymous grass from mouth to mouth
— with the Stones up there in colors
driving the shingles of our minds —
then the minds gone, the blood left only,
in its faultless beat, neck loose at collar:

and the leaves nearly all fallen,
no more air for the leaves to float down through
as if they were falling inside aquaria,
slowly, inside water, and we, looking out at the bowls,
or into the zoo from the cage which is this house,

and yet it is raining and the leaves
are riding the rain to their last destinations
the birds are trying to hold the air up
as they fluff into a thickness many times themselves
or burrow under leaves, throwing them up in the air

        like some mad dunsinane

advancing on us, advancing, and about to engulf us in some storm
like waiting in the wings of some incalculable destiny:
there is the bare tree under my window where the turkey-vultures sit
and the hierarchy of death is renegotiated
        every time a flight lands or departs

    sitting with their red faces out like dog-prick out of sheath
      we could call them dog-birds, didn't Egyptians once
        and when they go they are like crazy black organs
          quit of the body    and given wings. . .

I recall you are sitting next door, or could be
the times of your absence and presence being confused,
I recall that I could go to you there
        to be held and taken in
and that there'd be no great trouble in opening and breaking through

(it is us wanting to be held and taken in —
but what is it for you women we men are
some of us you know trying to find out,)
or do we go beyond, to the internal seduction
of the getting or gotten together
the begetting of one upon the other:
is it possible to put oneself out
of the knowledge of a separate going in and gone into
with the juices of a long *jouissance*,
and, with the noise of, the lovely
come of wave on shore, the slap of it,
the slap of flesh wet on the surf,
not know seducer from seduced?

but I look out there at the few leaves on most of the trees
and at the one bare tree that has not had any leaves at all
and without the glasses all I can manage to take in is the waiting,
the hunched black forms of music on black staves.

## II

He falls asleep behind her eyelids, she falls asleep behind his,
snow geese fall on the waters, soot brandts and canadas,
from all over the roads of sleep they come, some fast, some slow,
some frontally, some in long lines like Dante's cranes,
and above bird-peace the whine of war cuts high
through sleep and drones to stillness.
Closer bed, the far thrush settles, homes to bird-city,
the cardinal bleeds in a whirlpool of hot flight.

The road leads him in spirals round and round into the city,
the long road ribbons him out into position on its reel,
spooling him into the city, feeding him through tunnels,
over bridges, through funnels, and into the great maw at last
with the right hand   like a bowler's fist. . .

He licks the iodine out of her seaborn ear,
the sea-snail from her nostrils, the brine from her inner mouth,
he lowers himself to her breast to taste the milk of the seasquirt,
he lowers himself to her thighs and laps them like an otter,
like a sea-lion he laps the algae of her back:

She is beautiful behind the counter in a roadside café,
with belly pouting and Powhatan face with black eyelids,

she is beautiful with a mustache in a young woman's face,
he is fed into her body like the instructions of sleep,
he dances the dance of sleep inside her clearly, "like a foetus" –

    he who brings war and scandal into the epic,
    who plots excess of Troy and Babel,
    who asks not of Atlantis whether she is willing to fall
    or probe the mess of language into which we've drowned:
    profound sargassoes where no one comes and goes,

    her stance in answer, awkward on the tidal stair,
legs akimbo, asking answers – thighs akimbo answering questions,
    arms gawky beyond belief in the first moves of sex,
her breast divided – one star points East, the other West
    the guiding star split down the middle ridge:

but the sea does not divide its waters despite the cutting currents
churning the waters this way and that, churning the waters,
    despite fish-travel   exiled and homing,
    going up-flood to spawn, up flood to die
       over the walls of sleep

    SHE IS A LADDER, LEADING TO PROPHECY

    and birds walk along the road of forgetting,
    and man flies down both sides of the Atlantic:
they come from the walls of the sea, where land crumbles into water,
where the weary giants on either side fall down into the ocean –
they have flattened the cliffs into tables from which they leap,
the doors on either side of the sea flattened like springboards,
and in the sea they entwine their limbs, moving the giant tides
    from one hemisphere to the other, one end to the other of time.


**SECTION: THE KITCHEN (11): THE JUBILATION**

        She is the muse of my life
        on whose body I have written my poems
        as my seed shoots into her nostrils
        everything begins to breathe

    Ocean of Beauty   Ocean of Beauty   Ocean of Beauty

or else
　　　　that part of beach we stand on
corridor
besides which peace (left) besides which peace (right)
and in the center. . .

I said suddenly I understand the still small wind
I said it's fucking the sea in its heart
speech and making love
　　　　God talking and coming in her nose

　　　　　　　　　　What's the *dif-*　ference?

Where she parts the most
　　　　　　　　his or mine
　　　　　　　　　　　it's all the same?

## SECTION: THE ARTEMISION (1)

*Virginis os habitumque gerens et virginis arma.*

Aeneid, I, 315

Forty-four years I dream of front rows
filled with a single light, in the central seat,
forty-four years, the central seat is empty, forty-four years,
I know the day will come, the day will come when I least expect it,
the most difficult thing is to avoid forcing time:
forty-four years to see your face emerge from darkness, and
you expect it neither / you expect it not at all / coming from,
          coming from the place where you are going.

                              In the snows,
seeming-Russias of snow about your ankles,
about your elbows gaunt on a day of scarecrows,
          like that figure nearby,
                    cousin, perhaps, looking away,
and bringing out your solitude, your look, intent on day to come,
forty-four years in another life you have not seen as yet,
                              in the snows. . .

I am to recognize you from a thousand,
I am to pick you out from the unborn,
those: precisely without a face as yet, limbs, voice, a spirit,
without the lineaments of voice, without desire,
the wind tucking your beret into your hair
in those seeming-Russias, that perhaps Europe you say is Greece,
bringing you in some years,
twenty-four, twenty-five, twenty-six perhaps,
to that point in the photograph, to my point then,
                              involved in other matters —

     I am to recognize you

          MAGIC TWIG, FORKED TWIG
          radish, soul fragment, shard of spirit,
          break in the snow through which you shine
          black in a coat of astrakhan.

25

Two pictures, three, four pictures — in one series — shot
within moments of each other, reconstituting:
the movie of your face, the look
you dart at me as Arrow-Bearer, Diana, Artemis,
    forty-four years and still counting / time ebbing away

The trees are bare about you,
the trees have no leaves about you, there is
no kind of Spring in the air, but perpetual Winter —
desire is in the freezer,
your love is in the freezer of the snows,
forty-four years and the front row empty.

From Greece you move, from Delos to Manhattan,
with many places in between to be mapped out later,
from Aulis you move to our embrace,
the conflagration of our bodies already in the air,
when there is no sign of marriage yet in the stars,
Diana, Artemis — and you turn me to hound, you
turn me to hound in the bright courses of your mind and I
lap your secret hairs like a hound,
in the little wind where you stand, like the root of a soul;
from there you move towards Manhattan,
and on the nineteenth of May of this year,
at something like seven p.m. in the deserted theater, in the front row,
there being no one else about at the time, no one else having yet arrived,
except J.R. and he is sitting on the steps of the stage,
into Manhattan you move and I walk in with my boots in my hand,
coming from lifetimes in the after-life,
    a strange dog coursing after Artemis.


## SECTION: THE ARTEMISION (2)


In the cathedral loft, where they printed Bibles with spirit letters,
with the black letters of spirit, your face in a lover's arms,
in the huge loft which spreads your life before me,
your face in his hands, among flowers, your
face which moved a thousand wars in days of yore, which moved
a thousand to perdition, moved
sands along shores and shores out of embracing seas, into the land,
which founded classic cultures, a face which drove
men mad on desert sands, where your life is spread:

26

I enter like a dancer,
tall dancer unsure of his cue,
move a few paces into the joy of your face,
am undone back to the first kiss in my bathroom at home,
when I turned away, unsure of myself

*ATTENZIONE      L'ARTE CORROMPE*
                *attenzione, attenzione,* in a soft Italian voice,
around the corner from where you live in Little Italy,
                at the roots of Manhattan,
the loud voices of Italy in the wind of seeming-Russias.

On May 20th, sleepless the night before,
sleepless
            and full of whiskey in G.Q.'s apartment,
sleepless
            and full of knowledge in re your revelation,
with the photos still to come, the gift of images,
like a sheaf of corn, Artemis, like a sheaf of barley, Diana,
I the hound of your existence, with pads of silver, running,
silently towards you in the indefatigable night —

On May 20th, against my better judgment, I call your voice,
your voice is pronto to come out into the streets and meet me,
we meet among books and in the Vienna woods so-called,
send both poems to the winds, and inquire about each other's lives,
and I am drowning in your eyes, as we inquire about each other:

Twenty-nine years ago you were born,
you were born in a concentration camp on Delos, in the Aegean,
twenty-nine years you were perfectly born, in every limb, crying.
Twenty-nine years, you drank no milk, Artemis,
all those years you made nothing but blood and changed men into hounds,
alone in the wind of the moon, in your seeming-Russias,
with the snow about your chin,
staring into the distance for the meaning of your discontent,
your discontent preceding you as you coursed through the frozen wastes:

Your face shifts an inch in the picture, your face shifts to forward
from an almost full forward stance, your face shifts to full forward
and your eyes dart out like the eyes of the Arrow-Bearer,
Artemis, moon-witch, daughter of Aegean pirates,
pirates with white beards and the cloven feet of stags
pounding the forests of the Thousand Mountains:

27

O small country of your back,
where your kidneys ride in the wind, dry of milk,
where your kidneys distill the juices of longing
and you break in yellow waters
and I am the loam of a river bed
through which you run at a standstill.

*ATTENZIONE     L'ARTE CORROMPE*
and you have worked in the art all your life:
we shall make haste into this parturition.


## SECTION: THE ARTEMISION (3)


Because there is a man waiting for you,
because there is a man waiting for you back in your loft,
because behind your life there is a shadow —
                though we run in step, though we walk
                exactly in step, and soon arm in arm, and soon
                body in body, and we say, almost at the same time,
WHAT IS THE MATTER WITH US
    IS THAT WE ARE FALLING IN LOVE WITH ONE ANOTHER
in the smooth stream of love, with the perfect unison of a forked twig,
towards the violets I didn't pick for you at dawn
                and which have grown by noon:

                O MAGIC EYE-OF-GOD FROM MEXICO
                your country given away to the weasels,
                your country transformed into light

but we are walking in circles around the house, wondering,
if that lunch took place, that lunch out of *La Bohème*,
during which our shoulders moved closer together
until at night I put my arms under your breasts
and you leaned against me with your full weight,
and we are wondering
whether this is the time for our bodies to come together,
I am lying beside you on the bed, I think you came to fetch me,
there is a dowry of clothes between us, a snowfall of sheets
and you place your hands on your foundations
                as I attempt to touch them:

You wonder about the bodies,
about the fit of our bodies,
and I wonder at my capacity,
you are passive, your hound at your feet,
you will not stroke your hound,
you say you have not touched yourself: it does nothing for you,
you must be woken from the snows.

We are bedded in the South, among the dews of blessings,
we have our male and female fears,
and we spend many hours talking, looking for recognition.

You have a back on you like a racing mare's,
you have a front on you smells of mountain-lion,
you are afraid of your legs,
you fear your legs are too thick as they rise from thick feet,
but I say you begin like a tree rising solidly into this sky,
you rise from the bole of your tree into elegant branches,
your nipples: small berries in the mouth,

and it turns out you have your blood cupped in the moon,
cupped in the moon's month, Artemis,
and you are not sure whether I am a carnivorous hound or no.

It is four in the morning before the clothes are torn,
before the sheets are torn through and your blood flows on my tongue
as we grapple in a storm of agreement,
and it is four in the morning of May 25th, birth of our covenant,
it is four in the morning before our cry of recognition,
and at five we lie back with unearthly contentment
as the light plays over the branches and the exile is over.


## SECTION: THE ARTEMISION (4)


We came out of the city night, out of Manhattan at labor in your belly,
and I took you into the countryside where I calmed your suffering down,
we made love under the stars of my forest again —
I found in you requests no other woman had made of my acquaintance
        and which you said excited you strangely —
                you bit your lips to the blood.

                    Into the eyes of my friends
                    I took you into the eyes of my friends
                    on May 29th, woman of branches,
                    woman of ramifications, Artemis-Diana,
                    I took you into the eyes of my friends
                              and they smiled as if the sun had risen.

We are grossly in bed together: our first animal love,
we touch each other's fingers to each other's senses,
we smell each other like dogs, exalted to dogdom,
you crawl — bitch with soft flanks — soft stomach looming,
spelling the weave, rocking backwards and forwards,
then settle, baying, bitch at the heating moon.

Artemis-Gemini, Artemis-Mutable, Diana of the Heavenly Twins,
coursing the Russias of our minds / steppes / towns you have never seen,
I tell you Petersburg, Novgorod, the willows weaving
outside of Novgorod, the air brash with mosquitoes
and the bells growl in distant Lithuanias for our bridal
while your Greek wolves are howling at the moon.

Dog-Cancer, Dog-Cardinal, Dog-Water, Sirius, lapper of moons:
I drive my tongue like a plow in the fields of your back
and the adorable names roll out like the Zodiac signs.
You say you love the names we use, speaking with tongues,
you say you love the fit of our bodies, our reeks and odors,
and I am like cream among your milks and the splash of your blood.

Forty-four years for your long blonde hairs to part among my fingers,
forty-four years and twenty-nine of yours,
old man out of my depth, old dog among your freshets,
but we are the perfect fit selected by this poem,
we are the fit selected by the landscape we roam at will,
talking of children protected in the far home counties.

I will wait for you,
          I will wait patiently for you as others have waited for me,
O how I know the pain of those who wait now, who have waited before,
as you disappear into the snow and hail (no forwarding address)
          to fetch your freedom and mine
where the shadow has gone for refuge —
          and I take you into the eyes of my friends
          and they smile though you are absent,
                              as if the sun had risen.

## SECTION: THE ARTEMISION (5)


It is possible we fell in love too fast, you and I,
It was beautiful that moving together from the beginning
                                        as if inside a single body,
so that we could not breathe but together, step but as if together,
come unison — or look out of the world from the same pair of eyes
            and sigh in single exhalation / o but that BUT:

Now there is work to do:
                        we return: from the body to culture,
                        from blood and milk to culture,
                        from the planets' decrees to culture
and it is almost as if we doubted for a moment
                                        but the fit is too good.

Culture, Artemis.
Artemisia, my Western Star.
New Mexico mesas, night-moon-cure / plant
for dysmenorrhoea and gated parturition.
Crowned in the month of June with Artemisia, Huixtociuatl,
in your adopted Ancient Mexico —
and what is it in those Russias that have no place in this:
                                        functioning as
the never-never country where we meet, blinded by snows?

On the mesas,
in the Sangre de Cristos, after white deer,
in the Sandias, after white horses
climbing like the moon among snows,
in the hills above Taos where all the birds of Winter
meet in a knot of June — the wedding far from home,
in a previous incarnation of yours, far back in her dead eyes,
seeing in the shape of those eyes,
                        the great wide eyes to come.


                        But I am the same, Diana,
I, brother Apollo, in Dog-Star, in Crab,
pursuing the phantom of romance as is the way of my kind.

This is the lock. I am the key of light.
I ram into the sliver of darkness.
                        the fit is good.

You are virgin to me. You are virgin to yourself in relation to me.
You make me a virgin in relation to yourself.
                              You renew: fucking in blood.
This is the latter day of Artemis as Virgin,
                              this is the day your hounds
course you down into earth, Actaeon in the lead.
Your hounds trample your belly, leaving their spore,
their pads imprint your belly with prints of ice,
your white belly drowns in a world of snows.
What we must both go through: culture / what impedes and unites us.


                    Do not, Huixtociuatl,
do not give in to jealousy, woman of branches and ramifications,
do not keep me too close,
except to hold me inside you when I am inside you,
do not / keep me from moving in the world
                    / because the fit is good,
forget that *hembra* trick, those links and bonds,
and rest in the pillars of this Artemision,
one mesa of the Sun that will not fritter away:
the dog runs most yours when freest, Artemis!


## SECTION: THE ARTEMISION (6)


We must spend time apart,
we must spend time in the wings of each other, off-stage,
we must be patient: all will be well. I am in the woods.
*Estoy en mi patria de los chipes,*
                    my motherland of warblers,
Spring after Spring without fail: Actaeon Birdwatcher,
(explaining)
            *son las mariposas del mundo de las aves, querida,*
butterflies in the world of birds.

The sun plays in the tree-tops where the birds work,
where the diminutive hunt is on for worm, moth, grub,
the sun draws the birds in to feed, they worry catkin and seed,
the sun floods down into the forest like a tide,
                              the birds come in lower and lower,
working at eye-level now, where I can see your eyes.
I am back in the deathless, at eye-level.


32

Parula. Sweet song. Black and White: close creeper.
Parula, Parula, Parula: in his throat America singing.
John James Audubon in his throat: his America seething with colors.
The Black Throated Blue: jeez, jeez, jeez: dark prince of birds,
with a splash of fair ink in his wings, writing your poem,
Black Throated Green, with yellow face, coal-streak across the eye,
Cape May like a shard of gold,
shy Tennessee, shy Nashville high up in his Franciscan hood.
Parula, Parula, Parula — and the lovely Myrtle with the sun on his rump.

The eye strays to treasures of Sweet May, and the myriad violets,
unpicked for you where you walk on Long Island I happen to know,
in some visit without me, with the man behind you, the lost in shadow.
I bury my face in the May and find yours.
In the violets, resting my weary back.
It is as if I were in the shades of your back and each violet my goal:
I swear soft into grass the lexicon you love.

Many-handed, you stretched your hands to me the other night
in the smoky bar on Houston as we met again
when you had come out of the North after many a day of worry,
many-breasted, mother of darkness, you stretched towards me,
moon goddess, many-rumped, towards me like a cat,
many-handed, many-smiled, with your mouth ajar
your mouth which has too many lower teeth for regular beauty
and you said: I want reassurance / you did not say it so /
but you said : I want reassurance

and I told you fantasies of coming to fetch you with a gun.

*Estoy en mi patria de los chipes.* You will think it an illness,
a strange disease. The birds come in from the South after the snows.
How shall they come in year after year in the same manner?
    Of course, they do not.
Last year, there was a mixture of Myrtles and Magnolias at one time.
Today: not one Magnolia. Yet the songs there are / are the same.
Behavior is the same. And: in their system: they are interchange.
They bring sun to moon, moon to sun: THEY ARE THE TRANSFORMATIONS.
    They change me in the same year to all the years of my life.
O key of light among the violets!
    Out of the picture on my desk you smile among the seeming-Russias,
in your grim visage, there is a smile becoming.
Forty-four years and we are still apart, but the lion smell grows.
    And I, Apollo, know my job better, day by day.

33

I will devote this month
        to the joy of living only,
I will enter
        the bridal room of the dogwood around my house,
I will join
        the dance of squirrels, slow between food and mating,
I will discover
        deep in the green of trees, tanagerial fire,
flaming like bowels as we make love burn,
I will let go
        erect idea, totalitarian concept — break
the present cast of work,
                        whole days devoted to other energies than mine,
        the terrible compunctions of the spirit,
I will sink
        into the violets, their wet, sweet suck, and their insistence
on themselves only,
I will make
        long poems in your name
                        I have not made
                forty-four years, and all this time in snows.


And all the things we are, you and I, brought to remembrance,
your broken speech on the phone brought to remembrance,
your inability to talk (the shadow at your back)
and our resolve not to cause pain, to let the shadow down gently,
to let him sink into his canyon at peace, dying of thirst,
but a thirst and hunger so slow he is hardly aware,
the poverty of dying this, deprived of your breath in his lungs,
of your weight on his loins in the night, as you retreat, tide-like,
as you ebb from his into your own Spring,
along the canals of the heat (in the distance of Boeotia),
new warmth entering you from the other side,
        and he will turn and go at last
                        leaving you free
and not over-exhausted.


                        I will devote this month
to the joy of living only /
                but, last night,

I saw for four and a half hours the war of childhood fought again,
the bombers leaving in the dusk, with Summer smells on the air,
engines roaring with dereliction, and the bombs
hung like the weights of love under the fuselage.
I saw Europe, and lone England,
the man taken at dawn, sighing,
looking out of the window and saying what a beautiful day it was,
was it not, as they stood to take him in the Mercedes,
I heard the statistics of dead and deported,
while the German-lovers sat among their hair, falling about them,
in a slow rain of dark and blonde curls and curls mouse-color.

         and today I saw torture on yr. own continent,
outlined in serigraphy against the papers you had printed
and the prizes given for art struck like daggers into the assholes of artists,
like broomsticks into the vaginas of artists,
         I will devote this month —

We must emerge from this darkness into our life,
we must at all costs cease to be victims,
how little a gap there is between victim and victimizer,
how short a distance away is torture in the mind,
and beyond the enjoyment of pain, in the desert's indifference,
in the burning sun on which the snows of seeming-Russias fall,
it was this in your gaze you were expecting:
that we should take the river at high tide in its meandering
and make the path straight into Spring among the bridal trees,
and be certain of our loving, at white heat.


## SECTION: THE ARTEMISION (8)


This morning, at full tilt, a thrush slams into my window,
falls hurt to concrete and spins upon itself —
long streak of blood leaking from tongue in a drawn bow.
Bird finished says the mind. I've saved before,
         and will not leave to cat.
      Make night.
            Make night in box and place in dark room.
              Pour brandy into beak to disinfect.
That way if he has to go he'll go in peace, in darkness.
But he does not go. Three hours later, I free him to the trees.

And this same day you call me
with your voice of shadows
and you tell me the past goes out in front of you,
                    the shadow leaves
and the future enters at your back we don't yet know
but with a lovely confidence, as it was in your first courses
through the forests of youth with your puppies about you.
Bathing at the spring of the year, flesh white as dogwood,
your eyes white with the white of flowers,
                    we will finish at ease.


June 8th.
One lobotomized mongrel
shuts all the doors to peace.
This land, agrees J.P., is in the hands of curs,
this is no polity but a cheering squad
for a flag whose stripes bleed off it now, unquenchably.
            Make night. Take out the stars.
                    Make night: where do the bombs go over Hanoi,
                        over Haiphong, over the countryside:
are they falling into the same hole,
that the country has failed so far to sink below the sea,
immemorial as Atlantis, a fragment in the imagination of Asia?


We are losing our pride,
poets of this Republic, while the bombs fall
and we discuss our salving metaphysics.
The possibility grows
that we will have to go out and get killed
against the tide of stupidity, worst of all human sins.
We are supposed to teach — take only that for one moment —
we are supposed to teach, say Blake, with the ONE IMAGINATION
and at the same time we are fed crass questionnaires daily
asking us to calculate the percentages of our time,
                    slice our imaginations,
divide them by twelve: apostles and Church,
whatever Church of Love is in our minds for this Republic.


The dogs of war are loose, Artemis.
More terrible than the dogs of hunting.
Their mouths slaver with blood, cur feeds on cur,
Mindless, they rush through the streets of this uncaring township
that could be an h.q. for a Waffen S.S.,


36

they rush through the streets of the metropolis
choked in its doomsday ads. and punctured lungs.
One lobotomized mongrel: king of the animals,
        has closed the door to peace
                / and dreams may suffer for the common cause.

What is the worth of a man
        if he is downed like a bird by his fate
gunned down to silence in a pool of brains
        his thoughts about him no longer usefulness
    grey mess for packs of rats and shareholders
        stock-grubbers in the world he nearly owned,
he has now lost, and all his kindred,
             to the tasteless rabble?

## SECTION: THE ARTEMISION (9)

"I have been given a woman,
she comes tomorrow in the pleasure of God.
I have been given a woman, unbelievably a woman,
she comes tomorrow in the hope of the sun
touching the birthplace of the snows
with a light of, a finger-touch of, ESPERAUNCE.
I have been given a woman,
she is solidly upon this earth of blessings
in the sweet smell of sage in the West, Artemisia, Artemision.

        EVOE. ARTÉMISION.
        ARTEMISION. EVOE.
        EVOE. ARTEMISION.

Her body is a pillar.
Her body is a pillar of resurrection.
Her body climbs like a tree,
her smile lives in the highest branches.
I have been given a life.
She has drawn the great bow of my life
where it homes over the seas to an Ithaca in my grasp only,
to the weaving and unweaving of the cloth,
the cloth of sun woven with snows,
ever done, ever undone virginity.

37

EVOE. ARTEMISION.
ARTEMISION. EVOE.
EVOE. ARTEMISION.

This is a beginning. I had thought it was an end forever.
I had thought the springs dried up, the freshets stopped,
the fish starved to death or the quicksilver scales melted,
the food drained to the bottom,
the blood frozen in the veins,
the quick flies of Summer sunk to the bottom, in the mire,
polluted, polluted and useless as food.
The birds of air sunk into water,
the quicksilver song silenced among branches,
the little feet clenched, fallen without a murmur,
the beaks foreclosed.

EVOE. ARTEMISION.
ARTEMISION. EVOE.
EVOE. ARTEMISION.

She stands among the pillars, in her photograph.
Her mouth is closed in one picture, ajar in another.
It is as if she were calling, quietly.
She is formulating the life she will lead,
she is looking for a partner.
But all there is is the silent coursing of the hounds beside her,
circling. That and her heavy virginity.
Her womb heaves with blood that will not flow.
High above her, the moon closes its gates
and will not let her bleed.
Her teeth are thorns: she rends the veil of this life.
One of the hounds begins to speak.

EVOE. ARTEMISION.
ARTEMISION. EVOE.
O TIME THAT HAS NO HEART EXCEPT HER NAME!"

II

She has not come.
A piece of the sky came this morning, never seen so blue.
Indigo bunting on the lawn below.
Leaps at a dandelion, lays it low,
aggresses seeds at head.

Turquoise back in bower of black wings,
neck: doubtful hues — then, at the head,
a blue so fierce not all the planet-rings can spring that blue.
And at lunchtime: a hummer among the azaleas.

> I revise these poems, I revise my life.
> Sweet country of your back. Etc.
> Ripeness is all. Etc.

I require transfusion. I cannot make this poem without her blood.
Artemis, Artemis, listen. Could not / cannot / can't.
Etc. (She may well *be* a shit.)
Sun in the shadow of her snows
shine out and spill with words (as Tem with semen)
let the sperm river to our sparks, revivify,
and crucify the high upon the low.
Gautama: under your tree: think again.
This minute must be saved: minute particular.

> I had union with my hand,
> embraced my shadow in sweet fucking
> and sent out of myself children X, Y and Z.

Fetch me that Deutschland wrecked.
FETCH ME THE WHOLE TEUTONIC WORLD,
my bride of old unanswering,
that I have severed from the font of life,
unmarried, un-baptized, un-womaned here
while Strauss sings his last songs in gorgeous voice,
sky falls, the Gotterdammerung,
hope falters, detumescing:
we have so little patience with our ills. . .

The wildest goddess in the pantheon
stands here as epigraph.
And Hera, Aphrodite, Io, Eos then?
That myth should lead into confession,
that prophecy should lead into confession,
that confessional verse should find its way in here,
and what is the meaning of this invasion,
this adduction of the CLASSICS out of place
this sudden seizure of Greeks in a HEBREW poem?

Anchises came to England in a hurry. Or blood: no matter.
Arthur kept all his goings warm and saved the Celts.
Milton survived to enter Blake's left foot,
then England died and B. came West to enter more than one.
This body-continent, this Western gate
is all we've left / "Shine, perishing Republic"
and she was from the South, a land of slaves
under this Empire. I move no more — nor further West
though all salvation were to depend on it.

O Shekhinah, what are you doing here, in America,
is there a big enough colony of Jews to warrant this
outside of New York City?

III

Here I am left, with gold vacations in my head,
as the darkness falls over Lithuania
and from the seeming-Russias the snow falls South
down Danube cornfields, to Thrace, to Thessaly,
to Little Italy with the sun shining
but the sky overcast / thunderstorm coming.
Artemis, lost in the woods with her dogs:
        the dogs have rain in their fleeces
            and tears between their paws. . .
I am going to fly —
            perhaps I am going to fly
and her eyes will be everywhere reflected
                    from the clouds.

*DESNUDO EN EL SOL DE MI OMBLIGO*
naked in the sun of my navel, at Delos, at Delphi, torn open
the belly of the goddess — and I exposed inside like a babe
singing lustily already, out of the gods, the hymns and litanies,
(a greater cantor in the land no one had seen or heard)
and as weasels carry their young in their maws when disturbed,
it is said that Artemis took the whore that bore me in her grasp
and changed her to weasel in an instant, so that she carried
        henceforth her children from her mouth.

She has a dark line through the center of her face, Artemis,
as she talks of the Maya in our life,
she has a dark line in the middle of the small of her back going down
into her mines of pitch:

we can say of ourselves truly that like no other race
we work with the stuff of our life.
Coriander and Chinese bocaditas. We do the stores,
picking up strange foods. I buy her a blouse with many pockets
to keep a heart in / and poems in the upper arms on both sides.


Talk about sex, deeper than sex itself, all complexes
cleared to the light of day and duty payed on each.
As the rain accumulates in the streets outside:
will she be Virgin again, the Artemis?
                              Will we see each other (ever) again?
Or will it all be over, far from me, in a distance as far as Thessaly,
in the central valley of Mexico that runs between her breasts
where her father waits to kill and I am alone again
                              with my dreams in my hands?


The intermittencies of love expressed
                              in hesitation of hounds
(as in Faulkner's *The Bear,* each one a humor, Lion to fyce),
the fifty-headed monster, the spectral hound bringing Actaeon down,
Melampus (Sparta), Pamphagus, Dorceus, Lelaps, Theron, Tigris (etc.)
                              one pounding forwards,
            others lagging behind as if attached to trees,
                              their timing out of joint,
the chase distorted from lack of common purpose
            and then the baying of the hound in the lead,
                              the speaking hound, his holler,
                  and the pack exploding together:
                              FETCHING THEIR PREY.


## SECTION: THE ARTEMISION (10)


At the crossroads:
her haunches of an ass, for lechery and lust,
trotting among the trees of burning animals,
dolls swinging in the wind, with their heads lolling,
whose grandsons worship the crazy muses
stifling women in nightmare, incubing them,
rapists in Central Park, abortion clinics,
screech owl at night, facing three ways,
pecking cakes among candles, the witch's portion,
                              facing three ways.

Great stag of Colhuacan,
she who feeds on stags' hearts in the plains of Arcadia.
O into deer she is converted, o into hind,
and Princesses, child-stifled, downed in the form of eagles
invisible, rake talons through the sand,
piloting sun from Zenith to the West, in Artemisia,
Seven-Snake (Maize); Jade-Skirted (Water); Huixtocihuatl (Salt) —
changed into bitches, wide-eyed cows, beautiful women —
triad of livelihood and witch's portion,
                              facing three ways.


Weasel burrows, making love three ways,
Moon-mouth / Earth-cunt / Hell-asshole,
nailing her head to a cross of willows,
I singing out of the gods, transform her, Persephone,
feeding on trefoil trinities, among wild hawthorn,
Lion-head, Dog-head, Mare-head upon her, many mouths slavering,
burning the pilgrims in the thighs as they move down toward her
from frozen North, beyond the Northern Wind, carriers round-and-over
                      cultists of legend, o Hyperboreans.


(SELENE/MOON) / (ARTEMIS/EARTH) / (HECATE/HELLS).
Can it be our dead one who is singing, falling to trap?
Drawn like a bow across my shoulders, as we stand back to back,
I HAVE TAKEN A SIGHTING ON DIVINE BEAUTY AND MUST
                    FOREVER REMAIN UNSATISFIED,
devoured now by the hounds of my desire who will not give me peace
until my stags' eyes close.
Troy fallen. North fallen. Empire, from Maine to Texas, given way.
Broken I thread the perils at the edge of this world,
                  endless periplum of my life.


In Manhattan, on the steps of the Public Library, I stopped to breathe,
looked at the throng which bore the lineaments of my desire,
and was still unable to see the one in many / the many in one:
intolerable lack of wisdom in Colhuacan, o petticoat of serpents!
        And suddenly I saw at the crossroads of Manhattan, June 25th,
all the strollers dying sooner than later and being dead not beauteous —
with the pigeons swerving overhead like the souls they were to become,
and I wondered at you, waiting below the river of forgetting,
for them to come in with their unfulfillment in their hands.

Deep in the mist of Anaurus the dark-pebbled
she saw five copper-footed stags as tall as towers:
she took four, leaving the fifth to Herakles (Hera's decree)
and the great stags led SHE THAT IS LIKE A HIND OF IVORY away
whose soft skin I wear as her impersonator dies on Center Street
and in the temples of Colhuacan, in her own countree,
    for it is said that the hind is the emblem of wisdom
    to be chased patiently through the forests year after year
    and captured whole, shedding no drop of blood:


                that the winds might remember their way. . .


## SECTION: THE ARTEMISION (11)


Forty-four years and it is inconclusive: forty-four years
                    and caught
once more in the posture of waiting.
You've gone to Mexico,
to the Lake of the Moon, where the Sun-Eagle settled,
I went to Boston — these States began and I am back,
caught in the middle of the poem, undivining
the moment we must write, woman of smoke and acid,
thrown past communication, speech, unanswered letters:
    and I move out again among trees
                to glimpse your passage,
the hound-rush through midday, the silent baying,
maws open with great cries of hunting, but silent,
and Old Ben bleached among tree-trunks. . .


Carried to the island which was once quail and became light,
born a day before your brother Apollo, Artemis,
helping your mother over to Delos out of the light,
easing the Sun through blood channels, presenting him
skyward, with his golden banners drying on the wind,
who was to fuck you in silence on his altar at Delos,
and make you shoot Orion at great length in the sea —

re-entering the womb to be born a day later
and to sit on your father's knee among old-men-of-the-forest:
*yn iquac nenemj cenca yxaoca,*
with golden bells on your ankles,
*yxamaca, xaxamaca, tzitzilica, tzitzitzilica,*
wrapped in your skirt of waters, on your way to die. . .

I will have, you said to your father, sixty Okeanides of one age,
and twenty river nymphs to care for hounds and gear.
I will have eternal virginity and as many names as Apollo,
a bow and arrow like to his: harmony of the bow.
I will have the office of light-bearer with burning torches,
all girl children with the moon's death-number nine.
I will have a saffron tunic with red hem, reaching my knees,
and as I don't expect to live elsewhere than in the woods:
all the peaks in the world, and only one city —
but your father laughed, giving you more than these:
saying: take thirty cities, and crossroads, and harbors,
and may your bath sometimes become the prelude to love
and may he whom you kiss enjoy his sleep of death. . .

Caught on the edge of forests, edge of a pond of light,
eyes riveted to beauty, long hairs among your thighs,
among the columns of your legs, this temple built to your name:
I as I guess had gazed on Nature's loveliness,
eyes riveted to breasts scarred with bow-whip and arrow,
nipples like coral among waters,
eyes as you see me, calling the hounds —
eyes turning long like a stag's, sing out of gods your praise
as your hounds leap to mine and mine to my throat:
and I die with your names on my lips, O you of the white arms:
>Artemis of the showering arrows,
>Aphrodite of the fluttering eyelids,
>In the fan of the wind of the Immortals!


>saying: take thirty cities, and crossroads, and harbors. . .

White-browed
Bright-faced
Swift-footed
Light-bearer
Far-shooting
Night-walker
Horse-finder
Maiden-soother
Young-midwife
Persuasion
Siren-songed
Rope-dancer
Torch-bearer

Peak-crowned
Lake-eyed
Marsh-bellied
Walnut-breasted
Laurel-fingered
Cedar-legged
Stag-horned
Quail-feathered
Boar-tusked
Wolf-fanged
Goat-thighed
Bear-pelted
Hare-footed

Found-upright
Willow-bound
Branch-wrapped
Hill-pastured
Hanged-doll
Dagger-point
Sandal-wing
Burnt-offering
Young-moon
Child-raiser
Hyacinth-bloom
Lion to Women
     of Wild

My Lady Things

# III

The wind stood still at Aulis, the wind stood still. . .

Nebeuein. To play the fawn. Larissa, Demetrias.
Arkteuein. To play the bear in saffron dresses. Brauron, in Attica.
Ruzein: "to make a snarling noise with the chops."
Artemis Laphria, Patrae: Iphigenia in her car of stags.
Phocea: human sacrifice alleged, on the model Orestes.
Halae: victim's chest sprinkled with swords and arrows.
But some say this took place at Brauron in Attica.
Sparta: Artemis Orthia, found upright among willows,
the boys collapsed, drenched in their blood and sperm.
Ephesus: the many-breasted stretching out to me in Manhattan.
Cheese-offerings of Sparta, many holed,
and the many hands caressed me in Manhattan.

I look at you in the bath. You say: fuck me please.
All day I've been waiting for you to enter me.
I look at you in the bath. You tear my throat of songs.
All day you look at me and say: fuck me in the small of my back.
I look at you in the bath. Your thighs run with milk and blood,
into river-nymph hands: your puberty.
You sit among willows on your golden back and bleed
copper among the feet of stags.
I say: Sister Artemis, Sister Artemis of the golden feet and wings,
break custom with me this night and entreat me with your loins
smelling of alchemy and stones. And you shit blood.
I look at you in the bath. And you say: you must not fuck me, brother:
I am tired of this pretense. I am Virgin, with Athene and Hestia.

I looked at Nature long and hard, her body nude and ready,
Nature at puberty, with golden hairs among her thighs,
and because I look at her preparing to take me back into her bosom,
she pretends not to wish to have me until her dying day.
I am the Sun pursued the Moon unhappily till yesterday. It is now.
I am the Moon pursued the Sun unhappily. And it is now.
O Artemision where my mother bore me among quails
and the wild boar trampled the foundations, and the bear came
through a prison of tree trunks to the wild fountains among your knees:
they called the goddess of childbirth on the ninth day only,
she went through the blood to discover my head
after which the Sun burst forth, drying among his banners,
and spread himself on the wind in his sister's eyes!

In forest clearings the temple-pillars rise,
it is impossible to see whether they are tree-trunks or marble,
milk-colored or blood-colored,
of quail bones or concrete.
There is a clearing overhead where my son drives fire
and the forests singe at his passing and the earth is discolored
but a new shoot of leaves and trees puts forth another Spring
and the Spring turns into the Summer of my forty-fourth year.
I go, singing out of the gods, Apollo of the Laurels,
with my sister among my thighs on the temple's altar
and I run with dog-swiftness towards her debris
and fall to her with a tongue so full of speech the heart confesses:

            Revengeful one. Very revengeful.


    and the wind breathes above Aulis. . .

## SECTION: THE INVISIBLE BRIDE

### I

*"I have turned out the light*
*but it will not go dark. . ."*

Once in my life, in her life,
Love looked at me a certain way with the look which doesn't lie
and I saw she'd been burnished to her ultimate beauty:
     I remember it was in the middle of something we were doing —
I looked up to say something light about some comment
     and for some reason / ah *what* reason on *that* night?
  THERE WAS THE LOOK OF FIRE
         as if she'd just achieved final illumination:
it was in the middle of something we were doing
             but the details escape me —

       Do not disturb this peace,
       darkness of the world,
       do not invade this house of bliss,
       this happiness wrested from the moment of life,
       do not disturb this hard-come-by,
       laboriously won victory over restlessness,
       don't rummage about in the furniture
       which has all become now one bed of peace:
           last manifesto of love,
       last chance on earth of this tradition:

and as I run out into the new, with eyes open into disaster,
along the city streets named with other names than hers,
          at the time of betrayal
do not even then / with the long scream of triumph on my lips
         scream of man turned to deer
         boy to prey in the eagle's beak
         woman to laurel in the sun's embraces,
         that scream of longing satisfied /
         hiccup of satisfied desire / orgasmic cry
do not disturb this peace     for the fee my words shall pay you!

In her garret above the city, love lies a'dying
singing the arias she remembers one after another
waiting for her lover to show up
           so she can rise and feel

the scald of love in her bones
               the green trees calling where they live
and, leaning on her elbow,
     she sings   she sings   she sings
               *RINASCE!      RINASCE!       RINASCE!*
(but is yet to perish),

From the century's lips my wife speaks out in her own name,
crying the lost man of her youth and all her gardens in disarray,
my children melt in the sun of another country
                         which is the country I have left
to come to this beginning of the deaths we have to die
          at the windows of this town
               bursting with cherry blossoms and chrysanthemums,
                    suddenly/suddenly, in the middle of,
in the middle of something we were doing,
the windows of the city full of petals and crying telephones!

They that have not learned the art of Life
how shall they come to the art of *Thanatos*,
how start into the magnificent avenues of their dying,
opening out from the city into their childhood landscape,
and then, as shadows darken over eyes and ears,
begin into the alleys of death, turning aside from the highways,
wending their way from arteries into small veins,
dead-ends, cul de sacs, circular plazas,
where the dark rulers of the world sit on their golden stools,
drugs on their lips, pronouncing fates?

You are a region of my heart, death of the small entrances
     you are the population of that province
with big round eyes like an owl's, ringed with longing
               and you run towards empire
               as you would run to fat
               your population grows apace
               with a growl as of organs in churches
               a bellow of morning choirs:
               your population is growing
                         BEYOND ALL HEALTH

Cold has come over the city like a fang on the skin of revels
but the light is still the light of the Summer sky
                         in the days of our prosperity

— all of a sudden I see my children in the sky
                            laughing and dancing like children
in the middle of a very ordinary day
and I choke as if I'd tried to swallow a mountain
            of loss and scandal
beyond the politics, beyond achievements,
the song in one's veins of careers and of remunerations,


AND AN ACID I CANNOT DILUTE EATS AWAY AT MY LIFE


I can hardly believe in human beings anymore
            I do not know how long I can maintain
      the credibility of life for myself
and then I remember the moment
      when Love looked at me in a certain way and I hold,
            in the face of a greater light beyond naming,
and I do not sink, do not fall, do not cataract, do not ruin:
I DO NOT RUIN DOWN TOWARDS ANOTHER WOMB TO BE REBORN
and I speak out at last with the voice which does not lie
at the depth where it becomes the voice of any man —

and I pay the price, Matron of the bright names of the Lord,
Angel of soaring birds, Queen of all that collects,
in the name of exile, selah, in the name of creation, amen:

to the rim where Love looked at me in a certain way,
                            and never ceased from looking.


## II


> "If one plate
> of the balance of the Law is destroyed
> what shall become of the other?"


We sleep
      and beside us at the same height as our eyes
      the buzzards leave their tree and return to it
windmills of the dark sun
      turning over the brightness and the darkness,

                        the mind's lobes
            now assenting, now saying no
the light and the dark like sails
                        revolving in the mind


and sleep the only death we die and can awake from
    deep in the smell of our mouths
            our breath of meat and vegetation
    deep in the snore of our nostrils
                as if dragons curled in our furnaces,
                        while I am busy dying
the voice awakes
            out of the day's decay


I journey to the terrible foundations,
    the spinal avenue,
            outside ethic, outside religion,
woman under and above / man secured in the middle:
                I am earthed at last, I am rooted —
yet as flesh falls away
                I am become as nothing in your pit of bone,
man withers and disappears
                        woman shines like the grave —


The gates of the grave are below my house
guarded by the buzzard tree with its ferocious music,
nobody knows exactly where the descent begins,
where the pilgrims go down to the shadows of unremunerative death:
    but it is hereabouts — and perhaps it is under your body
            perhaps your great length hides it —
who knows whether your stride doesn't cover the pit
    as you walk in the dark air of my dreams
        and whether I do not begin this journey again in your embraces:


and it is a journey of birth make no mistake,
                though scandal and terror attend it,
        for all the sweet souls singing friendship around us,
I am manifestly that sower of pain I never thought to be:
    I don't glory in the role, very far from it,
but as the leaves fall in the hard rain
                in the never-ending Autumn of this life,
carajo courage claws at my loins and rakes them
                        inside the pit of carnage.

I would like to leave this house and go out into poverty
I would like to let the buzzards move over to a tree
exactly above the house and drown it in a white rain of loss
    I would leave these birds to their end
               and enter the embrace of the eagle
               burning in the midday sky
               consumed in a great dream of desire
and pass my heart through my mouth to his beak
               leaving my body on the dole of waters.

      The children present themselves in the far distance
          at the pillars of the grave in your sex
        the children at the gate cry and sing out
          in the piping song of their loss
        we have no father / we have no father
        BUT AH MY POOR MASKS
            your father
          fatherless himself
          motherless himself

*(Adjustment*                        *(One child smiling,*
*of clothing before*               *not quite certain*
*coming towards him)*           *if the parent will*
*(Glance to see if*            *listen or not/indeed*
*noticed)*                   *if it is he or not)*


     YOUR FATHER HAS GONE OUT INTO THE STARS
HE HAS GONE OUT TO WHERE IT IS NOT POSSIBLE
               TO HAVE CHILDREN ANYMORE

             *save only words*

I had not thought to cause such devastation
               and the secret of the fall around me
is that I require the excitement of carnage
           for the work I am perpetually about to do:
It would appear that I cannot move
           without inflicting suffering on those I love
I waste away in my poverty surrounded with words
I hear the words I utter preparing the Spring
          in the dying trees around the house.

We go out into the stars
leaving a sad cortege of mourners for our lives,
the children wheel overhead with the black birds of consumption
pointing beak downwards at the gates of the infernal regions,
the doors in the birds' wings turn over and over in their dreams,
under their eyelids the cities fall and the countrysides are devastated,
the little roots play among the entrances to the hells
    grubbing among death's foundations
                    with the still, small voices of new life.


## III


*"She has discolored my life"*


A breeze from heaven lets her feel her body
defines her outline and extends it
        against the shroud of my sheet.
In the grave's time
              in the same time as her age
she is a child in the arms of her own children
           and she has eaten the seeds
she has eaten the pomegranate seeds
              the week dissolves
        the planets curve into sleep
the sky is quiet and can no longer dance:
        she will stay below forever
ONLY BODY OF LOVE.


The roots of love begin below the grave —
              as love mounts up
the earth explodes around the grave
              the grave explodes
the body breaks inside, the mirror shatters —
            the great tree grows
Ygdrassil, the world tree, cold and bare
        with its massive umbrage of birds
and she cannot argue for herself
        except where she lives in my heart
she doesn't cling to my heart:
        with her hand in splinters,
           ferociously, the heart clings to her.

She dies
she has died many times   and yet again in the night
she dies/
            waking, with the familiar plunge in her throat
falls off the cliff of time with a lurch
                              the heart refusing to fall
and staying in the mouth, under the tongue
                              like a stone
to be passed into the eagle's beak.
Those that precede her on the brazen cliff:
                              I dip their names in night,
in the river of silence
        their names dissolve.


The great body is cold
                    like a river of iron
from its tip at the heart
                    to its hold at the thighs
the sword enters its cold sheath and freezes there,
                    the long body is cold in death
with a cold smile
                she stutters out words
                like a radio gone cold
she sings in fits and starts instructions to the dead.


She carries the body of death from the East westwards
                    though it doesn't know that it is dying
she walks beside the body of death, she sleeps with the body of death
she makes love to the body of death
                    going in and coming out, a good fuck-slide,
    though it doesn't know that it is dying —
        perhaps the wind carries suggestions of a wound
        the dead deer on the car tops still warn
        of this intemperate, pure source of violence
that cannot be read into at all.


She no longer reads in the book of life
                    former news of her time,
        the places have died she speaks of
        the limbs of the words move slowly
        the letters lie down on their sides and go to sleep:

the book has become a guide to the dead
                              and the lost places
        grey / grey / discolored by the sun
                              gone like old negatives
            faded beyond retrieval
*nigra sum*, indeed, night completely,
                *sed*, NO LONGER, *formosa:*
                              she reads in the book of dreams.


            HERA - HEVA - OPHELIA : ROYAL MAIDEN
            the snakes in the long stream of her death
                the snakes in her hair
                and in her maidenhair
                the snakes in her name
                before she married —
            I loved you once generation of Satan:
        where she had fallen into the grip of the winged god
        where she was covered by the diadem of feathers
        Unfallen Lucifer: that too seemed wisdom.


        And yet who knows what myths we re-enact,
                what losses without origin,
                what partings in what bloods
                and brooded by what feathers,
            what goodbyes forever in clouds of dark terror,
            what opening of the hand in what womb,
                refusing anything but the pure light,
        what unclenching, with what sigh of unspeakable relief
                we let the whole thing go
                without thought of redemption?


To know the end,
        the finality,
                        though one howl from it in the night
is also relief unspeakable:
                    to pass like a snake through the field
free of the slavery of bonding,
                to drop thoughts where they fall
seed where ground offers itself
                              of its own accord
        below the body,
to intuit the unending charity of the earth
        and owe her nothing
                        that too is wisdom —

Sometimes the sense
that life can widen to include the most
specific knowledge of another's death
                    reaches out to include
injury to oneself and the desire to kill in others' eyes
                    but those deaths do not
bring down life to their own level and belittle it,
    but rather death and evil can only be seduced into life
and marvelously eaten with the fruits of the grave
            through all space and all time: ONLY BODY OF LOVE.


                    — and yet the gates are blind .

                    and yet the gates are blind .

                    and yet the gates are blind .


## IV


            *"Bride of my body*
            *it is cold in the heartland,*
            *as I remember our youth*
            *it is my meaning to die. . ."*


A deep music devours time and slows it down,
runs down the maw of sound into this silence.
                In a traveling mist
like an orchestra stilled,
                symphony ended, a thousand voices mute,
sadly, as if attending at their own funeral,
    with a sloth of serpents loath to move in the sun,
the gods sway saying adieu to us out of their music —
to the hinds of wisdom, the owls of sapience,
the ten thousand bird-systems: model of color and songs,
the ten thousand fish kinds in the ocean of vision:
            adieu / we will come again when you can handle us
when there is music to delight us in your harps
        and your bodies can move harmoniously
                to pace and dancing:
we will stand behind you (as our prophet said)
            and you will see us before you also,
recognizably, not needing to be named,

detaching ourselves from the blue
tulle of the summer sky in Arcady —
as your minds burn with our presence, in their own kind light.


A stench on earth all pervading —
yet no one can find the source
it infects every house in every city
it contaminates even the leaves in the outermost forests
wild beasts carry the odor in their furs.
It is discovered to come from the sky at long last
from the remotest planet
(perhaps from beyond any planet)
THE WORLD BUZZARD HAS DIED
she whose wings are screens through which the earth appears
in all its sad regalia, with all its beautiful faces weeping,
the World Buzzard putrefies on high
and there is no carrion to eat that carrion
to disinfect that air


I loved a woman
but she was an empty building
through which poverty whistled:
when I spoke to her inside the building
my voice sounded a stranger to myself
and my speech
fell into exile.
Until I stood inside her alone, a house with empty windows
with that voice like another's music
to one who has written more than a single song.


Her hair was black
(*nigra sum / sed formosa*
a life ago away at Tyndaris)
her eyes were black
her body hair was black
as raven feathers, as the feathers of vultures and crows,
but with a gloss (the hoopoe's linings!)
against the dazzled whiteness
a sheen in which the whole world played in mirrors
and all the beautiful small faces smilingly faced each other
— but her tongue was crippled from birth
she could not speak
she could not prophecy

she could not tell, of either good or bad
anything usable — or if she did
much like Cassandra none would believe —
the victim city would flare again
against the dazzled whiteness. . .

I spoke to her at last
the voice was cool
the voice was irridescent
as a stream running far away, and unconcerned,
she did not think
she could make it back in her present mood
the heat would not rise ever again she assured me
*la chaleur / calentura*
the body would not come to heat, the juices would not run.
She says it is not a matter of love but of freedom
she cries that it would be a suicide of the spirit to return!
WHAT SPIRIT?
Shall the viper be said to have spirit?
Shall the hyena?
If there be no brooding
how shall there be a body from the first
or spirit at the last
to break the shells?

I will make love to empty air
I will spread open the thighs of air
and enter them with my sex of air
I will rock back and forth on air
and finally ejaculate with sperm of air
I will take her clothes to my face
and breathe the empty air
I will remember the pattern of the garments
the thinness of the material so close to nothing
that it is almost air
I will bear in mind the garden on the garments
roses of air with their petals of air
I will talk to the sky as I make love to air
and there will be more presence in this air I think
than if real women moved among these thighs
and climbed into the branches of these arms
which are turning to air
and putting out leaves     /     made also of air

Ah she may say the light passes, passes,
                              the light returns:
but there is some light I say that is lost forever,
there is a death of some light that cannot be reborn —
                    (she tries to rise on the air,
                    I begin my long journey. . .)
          Ah she may say the light passes,
                              the light returns —
and seek to give consolation, one's own strength multiplied,
          the world going on as if it were never to end
and you rewarded with more at the fall than at the start:
          but I have known light that passes for always
                              and never returns:
principal fate of light indeed     /     main fate of light. . .


                              V


                    *"She hangs in the mouth of Judas"*

The sounds of Spring, especially the birds,
                    loud and insistent.
     Obscene business of renewal.
I do not want to turn with the world this year.
     I want to be forgotten,
                    wrapped in cocoons of silence
          biding an inner time.
But — every morning the birds
                    call with greater insistence
          and there is nothing I can do save suffer them.

     Good morning.
          It is almost as if I could follow her injunction
     to work in the interstices of life
               instead of living in the interstices of work:
                    but then alone I've always done that.
     And to live alone was not the problem.

*Fantasy conversation:*
(Name): "I'm dying.
    — : (pause). Fascinating. How did you do it?
        Plucked out the feathers one by one?
            Plummeted down?
    — : Razor (.) Pills (.) Gas (.) Poison (.)
    — : (pause). Good. Hope you enjoy the other side."
Telephone call to friend or relative in woman's city.
Instructions to dial 999 and request ambulance.
To address x. etc., break down the door if need be,
the passage to the nest.
*Reality:* She will as well
       feel great relief
       and spread-eagle another man onto her turntable.


The letter is like a tablet.
       How do you decipher her short letter
       (She was always good at
            under-information,
       letting one fall
            over a cliff
    walking away in mid-fall)?
Light years separate her from her victim on earth,
and you cannot even hear the rustle of her feathers anymore.
    It is at that moment, I guess, falling,
     that I began the great wandering
      in the storm's eye, and that I entered
          essence of exile /


       How do you read
            the salutation: "My Darling (name). . ."?
       Survival of love
          or survival of habit?
       What are you to make of
          domestic preambles:
"Between two gargantuan bouts of laundry, mending, packing and doctors,
      I am forcing myself to write to you now
    rather than put it off on pretext of busyness":
         embarrassment?
  or the thing's so live another letter follows?
         BUT OF COURSE IT DOES NOT
   nor the next / nor the next / nor the next

Write the Ode: "She has killed Poetry."
( Instructions:)  she has killed poetry
   by taking herself away
but to write of the death of poetry
   requires exactly poetry
and that is: the *Elegiac Genius* —
and she has you tarred and feathered,
   whatever way she wishes.


 Ball-buster.
    She breaks rocks.
She lets rocks fall from her beak to the world below.
  Star-fucker.
     She fucks stars,
takes to her talons the great of this world
until they sweat themselves to a cringing,
      high in the empyrean,
 leaves them to spin among lost stars
    all by their little selves —
and they fail to find the mirrors of course,
   drops them at last like carrion bones
 and flies away.


      (and have myself
      in my own time
      & more than once
      held these same thirty coins
      in both these hands
      & may have felt relief)


 The interpretation of silence being torture itself
   and she inflicting it
perhaps not even at home while she does so
   perhaps fetching another,
perhaps eating with her great wings some circle of the dead

     we have not heard of yet?

# VI

*"O Queen Injustice*
*how widespread is thy kingdom,*
*give us this day our daily loss*
*our daily waste*
*our daily excrement. . ."*

Have been in orbit so long
can hardly quit it
the deathly silence
read as hope or despair:
cannot tell any longer /
nothing continues to happen
cruciform tablet
dark with a thousand could-bes
one or two meaningless words from time to time
and space to space
crossing the oceans as I had prophesied —
from shore to shore
shade of the shade of absence
not going dark
trying to make it / out of this destiny,
a weakness in the eyes
preventing it. . .

I think I move quickly: I move slowly,
I sit and stare,
there is nothing I want to do more than to stare
at anything that falls under my eyes.
I do move slowly, like an old man,
and put down my food slowly,
and stutter when I speak to certain people
(those who are close to her theme)
and cannot remain alone
for fear of becoming two, not one,
(and have been taken away   days I cannot remember)
for fear of becoming multitude
of people I don't know walking around the house

and talking in louder voices
than I can handle.

                  I have walked head on into a locomotive,
           it has flattened me against the wall.


    The night is exceedingly long,
                the day most short,
the night very short, the day:
"a century is but a moment in Her sight."
I am trying to understand the people passing through this room
when there is no one in the room except she and I talking
           talking
               talking do you realize
                        we've been talking
some thirty-six hours without cease?
               That skull, for instance,
owned a long time: the face cosmeticized,
    trepanation, five minutes go by,
as I break from speech with her, stare at the skull,
and say, after the longest while I needn't feel apologetic for,
do you realize we are alive and he has been dead here so long?
    and she says: did you never know him before?


Which is the way people pass, in and out of us,
as if we were laid flat and they were layers of us,
    but from another time, almost as if
     they were fragments of a family forgotten,
a family misplaced long ago, buried by one who had to return
    many lives later to the same place, to disinter them.
           She who throws herself out of windows,
              in the gyres of her morning flights,
    is happy with them also.
But I do not want to see anyone I have known in this life,
my heart thumps like a cold engine started up too fast
at the thought that I would have to open to someone I know:
to her shadow in flight / as she'd come in
                to batter me down,
    and look I said to her,
I wouldn't really *recognize* — and the scenario would be:
(yes she said, yes she said quickly, of course, I understand)

There are different sorts of people she said
        some are angels —
                            and pass through
    not supposed to be stopped
            on their way to somewhere I suppose,
O so beautiful / so loving
    they make a lot of questions for oneself
they make one ask and ask
                        // but in a comfortable way //
            you know?
and: what if all these people you see were but the screens
            — several beauty —
of one whose inner heart
        wanders forever over the earth and cannot rest
                asking nothing more but to fall
down through forgetfulness
                        to some new, unified beginning?


## VII


> *"Almost as if I were coming back to myself*
> *lost for so long —*
> *the long vacation from wisdom. . ."*


Returning again and again
to the inescapable theme of our time: *SPARAGMOS*, explosion,
the quest and wandering: going out, coming in,
    the waiting to be fetched / that passively /
                ultimate loss of male identity
        if need be to the hilt,
                lashed at by Hera, the everlasting Mother:
*Eli, Eli, Lama Sabachthani?*
                        As my blood returns into my mother's paps,
                    my lymph into my father's testicles,
            as I drip with the juices of their copulation
        and the witch waits among linens at the left of their thighs
        at my conception to take the sparks —
as I hang here, tongue lolling,
    nails falling out,
        wooden splinters oozing out with body oil,
            beard-bristles dropping out one by one like thorns,

the heart panting out the great cry of wandering
                    *Eli, Eli, Lama Sabachthani?*
            the eagle plucks out my heart through my mouth
                        and he goes out from me who is to wander forever
                            and stain the earth until my recognition —
I AM GOING, BUT YOU SHALL WAIT UNTIL MY RETURN


*Sparagmos:* the falling to pieces
                    the tearing to pieces
        of the world as body
                    the humors falling / each cardinal a humor
the survival of a few shreds and patches / the tatters
            to evoke new worlds,
and, below,
                    the bodies of the women I've loved:
        arched:  like white dolphins in the sea
            side by side like white rainbows

                            their fragrancies together. . .


No one,   ,under the appellation *"she,"*   ,reading,
will know whom I am calling anymore,
or praising, or disparaging —
                    all these loves of my life
    I yearn for equally
            for all their qualities.
Can one believe in the one anymore, the one and only?
                    But / by same observation
I mean I marry but myself, and give whole time
                to my own claim and credence.
Relate to others, working full time:
            who will waste so
this universe and time when he has found the task
    of leaving it   out of the very core
            of staying within life
    O more exceedingly than anyone alive
yet dying all the same, from the center,
            as if the two were possible / in *single* breath
EXACTLY as they are!


    When young, and tall as a pine in my heart,
        I looked up at the planets, selecting the brightest,
            and I said: I want life like the Sun
                    that rises and dies and rises again forever,

I want to shine during the day
                    and see all things of this world with my eye
        *VIDERE ET SCIRE*
and at night
            go down into the uncreated and sport in darkness
and in the depths of the sea, where Leviathan plays,
    I want the court of stars in my mirrors,
        the planets like eyes in my mirrors,
the great comets flashing through the deep, like bridal hair.
                        And so many years later
                            dropped in to talk with the Magus,
his dog, wary, one eye on him and one on me,
his fear at my black hair mixed with my silver hair
and the celestial fire in which I robed that day —
        and I said: show me in your mirror master, show me the sun,
            and behind the sun Rebekah
                bathing in Ramoth-Gilead, I knew as girl,
    I knew as enchantress on the banks of Kedron,
and he beat out
one thousand five hundred and ten years of my long life:
    I saw Rebekah and talked with her
                            then went my way


    And she wandered from that time on with me
but in opposite directions,
we would meet every hundred years in a passion of tears
but, as we met, sad parting was upon us immediately
and our caresses were spoiled with bitterness.
    She waxed and waned like the moon.
        I traveled with the sun, seductive to women,
        from time to time they took me for Elijah,
                        our male Persephone,
the wine quivered in glasses where I passed.
I was known as the green man,
being taken into heaven before my time
as the scarves of my years fell into the sea.


This ancient one,
    this unregenerate,
        so old time passes him by in the night sans recognition,
            so old his youth is as a caterpillar's
        thin trails of silk back in his memory,
            so old his age is populous
                with girls identical as day —

orgy of sexes thrown at his mouth, moon-gore of months,
   *odor di femina* in nostrils, insatiable groans,
and I said
   I shall be forgotten
      she shall forget to come for me:
         latter judgment and judgment after that
         but my place will be forgotten among rocks
         my cavern forgotten among waves
      she shall be gathering up the sparks to take them home
      who is last judgment herself, and how shall I be found
   who must wander the earth always,
                  beyond all history?. . .


Confused in the minds of my people,
last of my race and first of another race as yet unborn,
they look up at my falling apart,
   I fall upon the world with my arms outstretched,
   I am staked out upon the lower world,
but this is not a passion of sadism and inquisition
with which to saddle a civilization for two thousand years:
it is the taking up of the vulture into the eagle
and the end of all wandering in the instant of now:

      Rebekah bathing in Ramoth-Gilead.
"In the days of Abraham, she was called Sarah.
And in the days of Isaac, she was called Rebekah.
And in the days of Jacob, Rachel."
   In the days of Adam, of course, she was called EVE,HEVAH,HERA,
   Royal Mother.
And in the days of my. . .(name). . . ,she was called. . .(name). . .



## VIII


Out of the center, the King and Queen wandered,
                  garden of inner light,
with murder on the left arm, cultivation on the right,
      and they turned to look back
where they saw a garment of flame through which tree-trunks wavered
      as shadows in great heat.
The outer garment was a woman of fire
and the inner garment, when it turned in the shimmer, a man of fire,

and as they walked
she returned to the original fire, out of which she had been made,
     abiding with the fire,
and when the fire was male, she left the garment, walking out nude,
     dropping her jewels about her,
to seduce children who played with themselves in dreams
     — smiles on the childrens' lips —

and a river issued from among the trees,
    running through the middle of his life,
    the river was trying to find the sea
    and when the sea was in great cold,
    it entered the sea and was lost there,
    but when the sea was in heat,
the river went white among the sea of blood
     and was not lost in the wild waters
      SO MUCH FOR THE WATERS HE SAID
separating out the lower from the upper waters
    fixing the upper in the sky
      so that the lower cried out for reunion
       until the light put them at peace.
      AND WHAT OF THE RESIDENCE HE ASKED
of what shall it be built, the temple,
    that the radiance might fall from above,
      drawing itself in to fit the residence,
             and what reside therein?

While she that walked on his left resided in the Sea-cities,
rising and falling like a great bee on the wind seeking her males
    until the city of mankind fell in eternal ruin
    and she walked in to take possession —

while she that hung on his right
    lived among apple orchards, fetched out of heat at evening,
     as if a bride were fetched,
      and was set like candles on a table
       while the wine glasses quivered.
And she would go about in the times of his wandering
      when his name was Exile
    caressing the walls of the residence
     weeping in the mud and seduced
into looking after the children of foreign gods
     and would kiss its walls and columns,

69

saying "Be in peace, O my Sanctuary / be in Peace, O my Royal Palace,
         Be in Peace, O my Precious House,
Be in Peace, from now on, be in Peace". . .


        and going before him like a bell, with dancing sounds,
        she moved out of his presence onto the beast of burden, male,
        and from thence onto the beast of burden, female,
        and from thence onto the threshold of the palace,
        into the courtyard of her lover's priests,
        onto the smoking altars in the courtyard,
        and from thence to the roof of the royal palace,
        (the bedroom built in which they would unite),
        and from the roof she moved onto the battlements,
        and from the battlements into the city of mankind,
        and from the city of mankind onto the mountain,
        and from the mountain over the desert.


        Now he whose name is Exile
wept as the bedroom rocked under the weight of other lovers,
        asking: "Is not the sun
                        small enough to fit into this house
        and shall the sun's power be lost forever?"
                — and the King:
        "Why was the sun let into my house?"
"Nonsense," said Exile, "the sun shines all over the world."
        Whereupon the King answered
"And if the sun, which is but one of my myriad servants,
if the sun shines all over the world, how much more this Bride of God?"
        and Exile fell to crying and abandon
whereupon the King fell on his face and said to him "Master of Earth,
let me cry in your place."
        But Exile's weeping was unquenchable and he replied
"If you do not let me cry now
    I shall enter a place unattainable by you,
        and there shall quench my weeping."


                The Mighty-One-Sings
                The Holy-One-Blessed-Be-He
        Splendor of the Altar of Lions, My-Crown-Is-He:
                I name thee Kingship,
                Residence and Temple,
                Mother of Gods, Angels and Men,
                Mother of Animals,

and I name thee Pearl,
and Precious Stone,
and Rocks and Minerals,
Stars and Coursing Planets,
and I name thee Community,
Assizes of the Chosen,
and I name thee Cornerstone,
Bedroom, Altar and Courtyard,
and I name thee Moon and Night,
and Deer and Earth also,
and Garden, Apple-Orchard,
Light of the Sacred Well,
and Sea I call thee
where sports Leviathan,
and Holy Land Undefiled,
and Blessed Sepulcher,
and also Battle call thee and War I name:

They had moved from the garden a great ways,
demanding to be shown
wherein would consist their residence
and what their light would be
and of what wax their candles made,
and they caused the people to fuck on certain days only,
sporting the covenant
and the seal imprinted in the body
(where she folded herself into his flesh
like a seal into writing
and he moved among the pages of her breasts)
wherefore the people stood
with robes spread out over their children
gathering them into the holy arms
and Exile, who had waited all year
in the folds of the Queen's thighs
and glued himself like resin to her body,
when the once-a-year sin had inevitably occurred
sprang to the animal they had thrown off a cliff
to lure him off the Bride of God who wept in the mire
begging to be taken back into the light
into the bedroom of the residence,
and he ceased to weep for the garden defiled and his orchard
    and entered again the kingdom of his survival

Bathed in sky-dew he took her, her brother,
bathed in the oil of whales, anointed with ambergris,
in the fine smells and odors of the world
          and each time he took her
she rose into a higher heaven away from mankind.
Superb among the stars was his suckling,
superbly the milky way ran from her paps into his mouth,
superbly his mother fed him beyond his youth,
his mother fed him until his daughter lay
trapped in his thighs and he suckled from her also,
then the women went from him both together
      and he stood alone in his caesardom
                for above on high
                there is neither incest
                nor is there separation,
                therefore above
      there is union between brother and sister
                and son and daughter


and the feathered sky falls out of the sky
    into this winged world below
and all the birds die on the trees one by one
    their wings outspread
and are gathered into a great bird to be nailed on the tree,
      Ygdrassil: the world tree, with its great umbrage of birds,
            *Eli, Eli, Lama, Sabachthani:*
            it is finished the suffering
      and the way back is opened, towards the living day.



                    IX



And the men of leisure performed their duties
          once daily in prime time
and those who worked the fields twice weekly
and once weekly those who drove donkeys to markets
and once in thirty days the camel drivers on the silk routes
and once every six moons those who sailed the seas,
          while the scholar
      eunuch of the House of Study one whole week
    wended his way home precisely
and neither in the beginning of the night
          nor towards its end

but when the voices of the people died in the outer streets
and he could bend his whole attention to the Bride at candles-out
    then was the sky filled with rejoicing
        and the birth of angels rained like snow!


   As for the side which hurts our hearts
    specifically: in the name of the left
under which we groan,
    forcing the letters out one by one,
    like the eggs of the oviparous,
with amber tears, from sea-turtle,
  foam-born, to winged thing,
    female moth on the windowpane,
        gross gut of anguish,
    white male takes her from the right,
  black male tries from the left, color of vulture wing,
  but she is invested
        and he wriggles in vain


and I said: "Let there be Light," and it showered forth
but was wrapped in night immediately by the black moth,
brain wrapped in a husk as tough as walnut,
the husk spread out, another husk growing upon it,
screen after screen of husks to the outermost boundary,
the dark wine fermenting inside / the sperm gone bad,
  in the fading glow of noon,
  on the left side of their thighs,
  in the clean white linen turning grey she waited,
and from the marital sparks she made demons,
  inhibiting the wings of angels,
and the right was forced back in the heart,
    groaning to sing. . .unable to / and swallowed


    Peg of iron on her nose
    pinchers of iron in her mouth
    chain of iron round her neck
    fetters of iron on her hands
    stocks of stone around her ankles
    wine in her rotting brain
  dark flesh of walnuts wrinkling, souring to vinegar,
    the husband mutters in his heart
and directs his heart to the holiness of his masters
        saying:

I have not seen my wife in candlelight
not known her nakedness
not attempted to penetrate her blood
not turned her thighs to the light to peer inside
nor sought out the mysteries of her inner lips
nor turned her on her back to probe with fingers
nor placed in light my cock among her breasts:
          You in your velvets
you have appeared on the left of my thighs.
       Release / Release / Release!
This seed is not yours,
nor are these waters your inheritance!
Return O tide of dying wine, return!
The waves are calling you home!
In the Sea-cities, your lovers wait,
the bed of your passions is not this bed!
       Return into your Egypt,
let the Holy Bedroom be free of your groans!
Then I covered my own head and my wife for one full hour. . . . . .
   and ate of garlic which multiplies the sperms,
     arouses love. . . *et tue la jalousie !* . . .


   Tired of men and angels
I lie here on this couch of gold said the Holy One,
I recline among her hair whose firstborn shall deliver this city.
Then he scanned in her the Birthday of the World,
justly celebrated in heaven and by the things of earth
as they rejoice in the harmony of the most delicate number:
     — and I alone, among days, she said, have no mate,
        I, Day of Rest,
   but he gave her the people for her mate
   when the city had at last been delivered


          and darkness wept outside like a widow.



       X



          at the world corners,
on the four thrones between darkness and light
      where they rule from sunset to midnight
the beauty of their upper bodies turned to the sky
     the beauty of their lower bodies, to the underworld,

where the sun bleeds nightly into the waters
           she who took on all mankind
and she who took on only the gentiles
           and she who made love to our people only
and she who fucked Wednesdays and Saturdays only,
           came they from earth's outermost darkness
and sat for models of Hera-Matronit, this mother-goddess:

           Whereupon my Father
        made up from clay and wine-leas
     a body of perfection: bones, muscles, glands,
        shine of secretions in the silken parts
        and tufts of hair in the dark places:
        I looked upon this construction
    and held my nose at the stench of female kind:
        he knew that he had failed
        and took her away no one knows where. . .
        It is said that the night monsters of the sea
           followed after her,  ,lusting,
           rammed her into the rocks.

           Whereupon my Father
    wrapped me in sleep and took from me by guile
        a rib or dagger from the side
        no one knows which
   making the secret body of perfection over again
           braiding her hair,
    silking and velveting     plaiting the flesh,
        hiding the secrecies below fine robes
and, as I woke, she looked at me with a thousand eyes
           flashing like rivers
        held out hands to me like a forest
        and lips like the ruin of fruit

and the smell of her blood — far off, far off below the secrecy,
    was like the perfume of mountain pastures in pick of April
nor was she taken away / nor did I make a sign for her to go
        but cleaved unto her
   like a moth,
      square inch of windowpane,
        juice out through the syringe at morning peak,
          and by the evening this heap of eggs, and both as dead
as all of history, and comedy to boot

Lord, I am guilty.
Lord, I am besmeared with exile.
But Mother, out of compassion, goes with me,
and I do not wish her to return to you.
But my Mother is unhappy far from you:
I am asked to mend my ways,
to bring her back to you.
    Tall order, is it not,
to disregard the original complex? ! ! !

Then a spirit went out of the Handmaid of the Mills
and seduced the King in his chambers away from our Mother, the Queen,
and Exile united with her on the left and had his will of her,
while the King had his will of the Handmaid.
            How shall I walk from now on
            and recognize the path to follow,
            my children crying, out of another land,
            prayer robes empty, my house of wind,
            fields flat, untilled, no waving grass,
            flocks bled and sheared by strangers,
            let me cry in the night of wandering,
            going robed in storms and lightnings. . .

Where shall she find me that have been abandoned forever?
The two sword blades will not smelt together, the casting fails,
my wife offers to throw herself into the pit to save the casting,
from the depths of the earth I attempt to save the young metal,
bring it to birth like a premature child,
but it is said that I shall have to turn aside from myself also,
and cast myself into the furnace, melting my blood,
that the sword might stand guard over the city undivided
and my heart undivided bring forth the holy names.

Meantime, the King in his wine
commands wild animals and fowls of heaven,
commands the spirits to dance before him:
he sends the daughters back to the edges of the world
but they will not return and they die on his hands:
the sun circles the world, searching the sky for the moon,
circles the sky, searching the sky for himself —
a heavy stone rises above a tomb

                    and a widowed mother weeps beside it.

# XI

Inviolable though few
these precious months
this twelve-month of a year will turn my life
inside and out before we are all through —
while I am here, no one can take them from me:
remember that: to inform the house,
to occupy each life that trembles o'er the house,
each leaf of time, and that old language dreams
(this people's time)
fully and cleanly,
without a margin,
and not a thought to spare beyond the house,
being just IN the house,
*Domus*: that underpinning of the center:
FOR THE CRAB


Cruel mercy of loss.
Central. Complete. Self-complimentary.
As far as the earth stretches,
in / out, whatever fraction, part / or whole,
fixed, ardent, adamant.
They have been trying
to put us in our graves scarcely the blood run cold
they are already anxious to write our epitaph:
not only that
but to show us the writing
and cause us to admire it!
I am so far, so cold
they can only come to me in dreams,
they speak to me real close at such times
and come across to me.
At all other times, my affections and I
live at opposite ends of the world.
Will we ever rediscover each other?

I walk the rain from one side of the desert to the other,
I walk the wind, rustle the gardens on the periphery,
I walk the tempest into the city and out again
towards the other periphery,
she comes towards me with sun in eyes, moon in hair
as a costly jewel,

she has sheaves in her arms, and in her lap,
              lambs she caresses on the ears,
she tells me of time to spare as we pass each other,
              she tries to stop me and tell me her story,
the ARCHER, she says: we have nothing in common but travels —
    let us travel in each other's arms a while and trade goods,
              I need the pain she carries, the labor's growth.


              Alas pathetic wretch
              lost in miasma of romance
              aging day by day
              into a spinsterhood long as her life
        because she could not fetch
              nor sully hands with this reality
mistress of the last word she will always have which is "death"
        mistress of the last word she will always have
              though it choke her herself

                            which is "death"
        mistress of the last word she will always have
                            which is "life in her hands"

              to kill it as it's born.
              Suspecting my boredom with her
        she speaks the last word of death
              she condemns to the stake
        he whose spirit has already flown her empire
              she is the empty husk of herself
                            she bears no children.


Firefly in the night. Ah, stop, she says, at the last moment between
us, before our paths are drowned and we cross irrecoverably: Don't
you know whom I fetch: and whom it is I've slept with all this while?
—It is the Wanderer in the essence of exile you have slept with all
this time I have to answer; it is the spider you have cuddled all
this time, who waits for the butterfly emerging from the house of
fiction where she has dreamed in peace many years and binds her down
in his strong silks before she can dry off and breathe, fly to new
births. It is the worm in the egg you have loved with, the adder you
have licked, the salamander you've suckled; it is the rain, dreaming
of great strength in his birthplace out at sea with which to cover
the world and drown out loss; it is the wind that travels further
than geese in the night to wreak his havoc on the great cities and
bring down spires; it is the sun in his blood as he lies buried under

the ocean, the gravity of all things as they fall, the rot on the ground, fallen; it is the withering you have loved, the addled task in the addled brain, the drying out of the imagination you have adored, firefly in the night. . .

> *And she answers: Look at me, LOOK AT ME.*
> *And she pleads: LISTEN TO ME, carefully.*
> *PAY ATTENTION TO ME, with tears showing.*
> *You have caused me sorrow unto death.*
> *You have seen me awry and not recognized.*
> *And she bares herself, husk after husk,*
> > *that I might see inside her.*

The flames that were facing away from each other, turn towards each other and smile; the faces, true enough, turn back towards each other and embrace. Divorce is undone and remarriage occurs like the cherry blossom on the branch, the chrysanthemum in its cup of gold. Under her wings, in darkness, a pulse of light sends out the singing birds: sparks of music on the air, the birds, grey at the start of flight, acquire their colors like banners, the maggots shine under her wings that had lost their gloss and reflection, her feathers are powdered with gold, her talons shine like jewels. On the far tree, I am filled with blood and lymph again, I hang fulfilled, naming the jewels as they come, the birds in flight, all the emergences:

> I address myself as "My Son."
> In the old days had I not
> > named myself after the son I was
> supposed to father?
> Is the snake, resplendent in new skin,
> not the son of the skin he has shed?
> The world breathes in and out:
> I recognize myself in the dark,
> complete in her embraces.
> Hera-Matronit, O wife of old,
> We have always known the answer:
> > allaying the pain of what the world is
> from time to time
> > haven't we merely found it convenient to forget?

Child, have we not seen? have we not seen together?
Pushing ourselves beyond our strength,
> > have we not seen it together?

Pushing ourselves beyond our limits,
                    feeling we have killed each other,
        but also feeling each other warming,
grass under snow:
        is it not blessed relief to feel the grass
without seeing its blades as yet
        although you know the growing will be painful?
— And whom do you think it is, in your arms,
                    that loves you so she asks,
        this Bride of God you've been invoking?
and if it be She, then what are You, She asks,
                    both at the edge and center,
        and Whom have you been so blind to all this while?


                    Bones rising from the sea.
        The great white song of our people from the blood.
        Achievement of oneself, and of the people,
        together in the night in arms over the city.
        Continence! Continence! cry the vultures wheeling,
        the carrion-eaters over the city.
        Love! sings the eagle, his train of singing birds,
        Love! sings the seed in the ground,
        the metal in the furnace.
                    One by one the limbs,
        one by one, shining, in a white armor shining,
        one by one the limbs brought in, *Sparagmos* countered,
        one by one married to each other, arm linked to shoulder,
        and leg with thigh, one by one the wedding,
        one by one feels his blood turn the color of marriage.
        And the children sing: We have again a Father!
        and the widow sings: Love! I have an Husband!
        And the garden sings: I have an Husbandman!
        And the beasts take food and water from our hands.
        Shall these bones live? Aye, Love! Aye, Love!
        Long March is over in the night, Long March
        continues among morning dews, all's paid,
        receipted to the full, all contracts signed,
        the house is purchased that had fallen vacant —
                    as one by one the limbs
        rise on the air,     and tower in the light!

## SECTION: AMERICA (1): SPARAGMOS: PEN/INK/PAPER/PENNA.

While translating Scriptures,
                    (folk-tale, not record),
black-cowled, I imagine, mephistophelian
                    as the white devil behind him,
white silk and silver boots:

                                        PROJECTING

gloss woman shapes onto the walls —
                    (and he, unable to write),
mad, throws bottle — black/blood/sperm —
                    collected to this day,
scraped — mandibles of time — by tourists,
        refurbished daily by curators.


            Through victim village, victims, passing:
objects as similar to each other as the dollars they buy,
            along a row of trees, white body of paper
and, *habeas corpus*, (tree limbs, as of women)
            thrown in disorder along the paths.
                    Little astrologer,
with hearts for eyes, black hearts, coal eyes: INK:
            do you, he said, when writing, when about to,
do you / have to feel *fresh* or *tired*?
            and I said with confession
heavy upon me, whole day's, whole mind bent unto /
                    *weary*.


            We had buried that evening
drug culture.
            Next morning, day of sunlight:
the permissible body emerging everywhere, disjointed as mine,
walking with S.Q. on Eighth street, saying:
            This anguish: not being able to be
lives of all beings, bounded in by
one set of circumstances: that is (suddenly):
            *ECCLESIA*, the Church of the Dismembered.
She: ? — Well: He that is the Body of all things,
and nothing of Light coming to birth, save through Me (had said)
            bearing all that, with no surrender.

That the lives are in Him, or in His female Church, who cares.
For they needed, in those days, to preserve the male impeccable,
reducing in His Bride all the limbs of the Beloved.
    But: male or female displacement, it's all one.
And I / I will have to wait then / unable to choose:
to wait for whatever chooses me, coming towards
this life, falling to pieces in order to build another life,
task easy at last, smatter of patience, wanting but some
coming to terms with solitude, some letting time pass,
body turned to grass little by little, green and fetching,
some parts pecked out by birds, seed-lovers, other parts
                                    ACHIEVING LIGHT?

        On your body of paper,
            not, quite, dead, your, body, I, write, not, quite, dead,
        having admitted, this thing I have become, this writer,
        might be anathema at times, mere vomit in the mouth.
        And all Manhattan had to offer that day
        was a porno film between appointments —
                        breasts, ass, apparatus only,
the only WHOLENESS
            trees flattened everywhere by sheet lightning,
            limbs lying everywhere dismembered,
            birds with lanyards of flesh in their beaks
                    building phantom nests.


The initiation
        took place far back:
Albigeois country: skull opening wide,
doors sidling apart like an observatory's
virgin telescope erect at stars,
        obstetric cleanliness,
fixed upon Saturn:   rings, by God, those rings *exist*!
        Old man taken through his grades, long years ago,
        *Sparagmos*, last stages of falling apart,
                        shower of stars, homing,
to power. Fist of power, homing, that will,
                        strike soon, directly.


        Turning in dream night, the disjunctured,
bodies of my faithful, those in the far, buried, past, at whatever
may still be called "home" over the loosening earth, the heart,
too big, too big to inkeep, bursting with treasure,

as who would have children that would be words
searing the page like acid: sperm and black swim of words.

      But through Me. But only through Me, He said, laughing,
that consciousness of power in his veins.

      Let them turn. Let them present: parts of the body.
Lushness, the pastures of green flesh, her entrances and maws.
Victim I have not caused to bleed at apex of her month.

      I give all help I can.


      In New Hope, Pennsylvania, now, canal: back of my yard.
(My yard). Proud pair of sentinels, Canada geese, still wild,
parenthood passing, silent canal, looking to right and left,
eight olive-colored chicks in protective brackets.

      Morning passes. Tourists come in.
Souls of no country, owning everything. The trash waits for them
      in the stores: Trash = Dollar = Blood.
And they spend everything, everything, with no thought, whole pockets
on the trash they carry away, in eye, tongue, hand,
      coating their arteries like a slime,
                     never compounded of Light,
      held in no wise of communion.


## SECTION: AMERICA (2): SEEN AS A BIRD


The light in the skull of the bird
      tugging her down
            she'll fly by the rest of her life,
mirror of sky among leaves,
      in low grasses at morning,
         mirror of high sky in low and of heaven in high
            along the milky way —
her eye: the order of the heavens
        falling  /  falling with the weight of damp stars
             down flocks of other birds
             down through t.v. antennae
                   funnel of space
          above the house at last
            great fields of light above her
    over Cape May

Birds in layers on the sky
a flock of certain birds above a flock of others and besides
      yet a third flock
      kettle of broadwing on the spiral air
           cut to the quick by geese along the shore
                and here the blackbirds scatter like ink-shot —
the sky has great depth
      the depth opens on without end higher and higher

      Alighieri describing the major angels as birds of God:

      Take here the little birds for the kingdom of heaven,
      the little birds for the banners of God —
and say what we love about them is simply the system:
that they are all of one set, yet different colored,
      id est — diversity within unity, heraldic counterpoint
      of certain colors where others are expected to be
— my dream as a child, the interchange of colors —
      what gives my mind peace, my mind peace, my mind peace

      immense fields of light traversed by angels

              / / / over Cape May. . .

## II

Seeing her as a bird,
      looking within that mind
for the cut of our sparks in each mirror shard,
her flight breaks over and over
      as she tumbles down
      through cloud, through stricken dawn-dark, and bait and lure,
              TO
      if she be (for example) that one-eyed falcon, sparrow-hawk,
      bird of the year,
          so must in nest have lost
      one half of strike-force within the head
yet falls on sodden sparrow in his trap
      waiting her tear of talons and her take
          his cheep towards
          his and her father both.

We'll have, above all, her movement
                and her descent, layer on layer,
                                through the bright cloud of our blood
and the exact description of her rapine
                when she comes to fetch us
                                fingernail by fingernail

                I mean   of course   talon.

        Look long ago the sky had many birds
        look long ago the sky had many colors
            and now we have the chicken only
            and the sparrow like an aerial rat.
        We mourn like antiquarians for the world's colors
            while the rest of the world makes do.

### III

And she is bird, falling,
        and I am bird, passing from behind that branch
to this branch in front of your eyes, and you are bird,
        hopping to middle branches in a three-tiered forest
and he is bird flits to the first branch in the foreground of /
            your alien life under heavenhome:

        and they all mirror each other, looking with bright eye
        periscope to the shard of the inner mind,
        at the tone of your color today bright cousin,
        and the shade of your tint tomorrow, bright female cousin—
        and, by God, I think they talk, Alice would say that morning
        as she broiled the two budgerigars side by side on a spit.

        while the white heart of the sky, ignorant of all color
                arched over, archangelical
                throbs in restricted place
        the pure white heart pulsating where it borned
                with rims of mourning

            *Elánus leucúrus*, minute particular,
            Coyote Hills, on San Francisco Bay,
            November seven-one (great bird of God)

            goes into somersault
                    revised and held thereafter
                and, looking down —

buckle of elbow forward
drag back of pinions in the wind
slow crash at twilight angles —

( the planes in circles overhead, ever diminishing )

slow fall to grasses like the dying snow.


## SECTION: AMERICA (3): SHE TURNS BLACK


In the cities of Atlantis
at the bottom of an ocean of milk
in a light of milk
the children of Atlantis skate on milk
and the frozen towers
soaring at the blue sky
look down on them and reflect their heads
their heads only in the lower windows

and as the children turn and turn to the waltzes
they turn black one by one and the whole population is soon black.

II

The old image
of positive to negative
bringing out the black swans
from under the world
to sail along the pavement
and they reincarnate
in the tall Cuban whore for instance
with her book of men by her bedside
and her chamber pot.

We ask of those shadows
the heroism of
doing without the light
just as it shines on them
and remaining in their darkness
for the benefit of the whole earth
so that we can go into the darkness
and both light and dark emerge together
in a redesigned eternity

86

Pulled in his stomach they say    against the dark
couldn't see that dark he embraced    couldn't see it at all
    for his own creature
let it grow to independence    declare its independence
                                chase him around the house awhile
till he grew used to her
                    rinsed out her pots at night
got to rinsing her brushes
                            sized her canvases
    for the gold of vision
                    and all she had to do from then on was paint
                            but she painted shadows.

### III

Lying down in the dark    only the ivory of her eyes
she tried to tempt him into
    the archetypal American romance.
        But they came and said to her that she shouldn't go with him
        or have any food with him    or talk
        or sleep with him.
Their hands itched for each other but could do no more than itch.
        I mean man to be a woman and black too

### IV

On the night side of love
when I held the night in my arms
I mean the night I had forgotten I'd made and was my creature
against the blinding white sheets
as I pressed her milk out of her breasts to feed myself
    which was not black
                        I took her picture


and in that negative
where she delivered    the load of the colon was white
and where she took me in    the larva of man was white


        but the seed
        the seed of the white man in that storm cloud
        the seed was black!

                I reached in to take it back again
                        but the tempest was spreading.

## SECTION: AMERICA (4): SHE FLIES THE ISLANDS


Jerusalem fallen over the edge of the sea
the human city deliquescent
walls junked in a sweat of *bagasse*
one pound of sugar = one gallon of juice = a good retrieval,
the slaves sing in the trees like orioles
like charcoal grassquits
like the black-throated blue I found on Bordeaux
       after looking all over New Jersey,

She comes to collect their sparks at day's end
leads them through coral-bricked doors
in the ruins of ghost plantations,
as they shoot each other in the back three hundred strong
picks them from fathoms of dark water
takes them into the rebellious Guineas of their eyes
the unconquered Malis of their inner eyes

      She lights up the dark
      she generates light in the sea
      she rounds off the blinding turquoise of the waters
      she touches treasure with her searching hands
      stripes wrasse and tang   damsel and butterfly
      costumes whole generations of angels and parrots
      retrieves the irretrievable

      electrifies the deep

She is the poem making its way over the water
the poem taking on its own light and color
her black swimsuit slips from her
her belly sags into the open sea
      her breasts rotate   like anemones
      she puts on the body of light
      expels the gathered darkness like a squid
      opens the resurrection
         I follow the dark rim of her crater into the rocks
         follow the sea into her crotch
         I am trapped in her thighs as a fish among coral
         we inhale a new life with the sound of people dying

crucified on the surface of the irridescent waters
watching far down the mothering of pearls
measured the walls of the abyss
        into which we cannot ever fall. . .

## II

        Washed into shore at morning
        longing for sleep, unable to
        retrieving my darkness into light
        surf squeezing light out of the sea
        pounding the beaches with fists of light
        (roar of arrival all the length of alba)
        writing on morning beaches
        on fronds at water's edge
        on field of morning glories
    the sky stretching itself over the whole earth
    seeing itself reflected in the earth, and in love
        I fish for poems as she fishes for souls
        and men for the great blues of the ocean.

Ah Baudelaire   my like   my spectral brother
*you* knew there was to be no overdose of the Tropics
scarcely that. . . . . . . . . . . . .rounding of the Horn
                    that blasphemy of courage
confinement off La Réunion
                and afterwards
whole lives remembering there had been other worlds:

    systematically: to write the poem before the event in the poem.

## III

From the ocean floor
out of triton lips, conches, cowries, stars,
their pale pink inner feet   their pale pink palms
rising from reefs   breaking placentas of turquoise
rinsing perfect sand from their mouths   the white ablutions
crawling into forest with spider and scorpion
working their way to the crest
        where work is the hardest of all
        the cane cut round and round the clock
        turpentine disembowelled
        mango raped against palm
        the locust crucified and flayed

and hundreds glare down the dozens
until it's time for an end!

> Very convenient owning these islands now,
> rangers expound plantations dawn to dusk
> dim Stateside memories mostly at rest,
> visitors frown a little over. . .slavery
> and rap about it with "good Blacks" —
most of whom have the perfect lexicon of the British Indies
"The Crown oppresses us but with the Eagle we fly from shore

to shore / and therefore. . .God Bless America!"

Courtesy John Alden, Boston, Massachusetts
we visit the original Treasure Island
> *KAPITALISMUS! ! !*
crabs on the walls groping for light —

> Her feet are lost as the waters close over her shadows
> we imagine her retreating thighs   her head far down
> the bag she carries over her shoulders
> containing the Federation of the Islands
> the Constitution of the Eighth Continent of the World —
> in the rare waters I listen for her hands
> grope for the sound of her breathing
> where it rasps beside me

> (balled by the sea to our molten minds)

in the plane overhead no one mentions Havana. . . . . .


## SECTION: AMERICA (5): SHE IS A CHILD


I remember it now when she was a child in America
she looked down at herself lying her length on the bathroom floor
and opened her legs to the mirror
and from Charleston to Phoenix and on into the Bay
> the whole of ocean roared inside her thighs
> with the voice of her husband to be
> and rose and blossomed in her sight
> like an anemone of blood —

and from the distant shore
fires leapt out of forests to light the night of the world
the people running about with their arms above their heads like birds
    carrying babies

        and their arms were burning

## II

From the city far below
from the city at the mountain's feet
    the mountain of circumnambulation
the wail of sirens reaches up to this blue bowl of birds
    *pradakshina   pradakshina   pradakshina*
in quiet song among the branches
    she takes me by this hand
    and she takes me by that
    and lies me down in the garden of beginnings
    she lays my cock in the rose
        among the fingers of the iris
            between the lips of the lily

    I cannot go in
    I cannot go in past a certain point
    she is too small
    too long and far ago
    she is too shrunk
    backwards backwards backwards
    into the dead with no name
    I cannot enter her small thighs
    her buttocks hardly fill my hands
        no larger than apples.

First *tantra* in the hardening light
    she remembers how he stood above her that had given her days
        and his fists are like the pummels of two swords
                tight at her shoulder blades
    his lips like an iron bite around her lips
    the *sutra* of his tongue in her mouth
            like a dirk of flame

    O bright lady of scholarship
    sum of the harmony I cannot see
    *dueña* of knowledge
        *daikini* of the sea under the wide blue wind

I want the armpits of sixteen
I want the curve of seventeen at the rims of my palms
I want the weight of eighteen bending my fingers back
I want the nipples of nineteen in my eye sockets

I want to teach freshness

### III

The Schools
the great Academies of America
are bursting apart like pomegranates
of their own weight
    and all the seeds float away over the mountains
to become the child brides and bridegrooms of the teachers
    for if you do not meet your children on the field of the body
they will not be able to go forward from you
    you will be meeting them in sterility only
postponing history
                at the latter day
                      causing a hesitation

              perhaps arresting it.

The Schools return in ever diminishing circles
        to the mouth of the silent womb
language runs down and knowledge on its knees
        crawls back to its original source
the first teachers teach in fiery unison
        and all the subsequent teachers are stricken dumb

I shall appear at your mouth little child
               with my lips at your lips
               we shall give birth together,
you to my head as I emerge into this garden
I to the words you say concerning this garden
we shall say: look world   look world   it is very late

          In the first *tantra* of the burning earth
          the father is a child again at his daughter's feet
          he learns his parts and happiness rehearses
          sometimes he reaches up to catch a breast
          sometimes he sings a little song aside
              sometimes he suckles.

## SECTION: AMERICA (6): SHE BECOMES OUR LADY


For our reading pleasure she invites us now
to take this poem with us as we deplane
at the southern fork of the coiling river
which ends by flowing North
                    through the golden womb of the Lady.


                    I took thee for thy better
                              loved thee not
                              get thee to a nunnery
                              make it quick.


        *Les vaches laitières*
from confirmation to marriage
        with nothing in between
                    but the bleeding months,
wasted prairie out there, laid flat by crush of seasons
                    bellowing bulls in frozen fields.


Milch cows of Illinois and Indiana
                    with their oval faces
hot tongues working round their dentures
                    the placid working of dentures
                              from side to side
and the eyes in which you drown
                    the deep maws open
whereby you measure the sizes
                              of their milky ways


Well I shall prefer them nonetheless to the great bitch of New York
                    the bitch and gabbler
              who wears her cunt on her lips and goes
              yatter-clack, yatter-clack, yatter-clack
          but she talks about freedoms she has not attained
oh interminably she talks of all the revolutions she has not been through
                    and her legs are locked


                              *O these ideal types!*


So they gave them
        whatever it is they wanted
              in the shape of things men usually want,

that is:
  sports-buses
        electronic shavers
            telephoto record-players
                stereo cameras
                    long-wave telephones
                        a.m. & f.m. stamp-albums
                    macro and micro rifles
                acapulco greens
            go-go girls who stayed put
        an occasional whiff of our Lady
    as she minces to Mass
but they'd have none of them. . .

(ah. . . . . . . . . . . .COWS you like to screw?      *Ach so. . . Ach so. . .*)

## II

The generosity
of the old-world systems
the exhausted systems
which have seen universes explode / fall by / and fade
              each with their doctrine
ah they're good at telling a religious temperament from a distance
              even when blasphemous
knowing the Lady's arms will enfold at last
              (and in her Jewish form what tho' what tho')
all the dissenters, all the dead.


You shall not my daughter wear patent shoes
you shall not my daughter stand over clear or even muddy puddles
you shall not my daughter take baths without powdering the surface
you shall not linger while wiping your ass
you shall not loiter with the paper between your lips
you shall not litter your torsos with sleeveless blouses
and you my son shall not let Jesus out of your body
unless He be received into your properly constituted marital corporation
o my daughter.


And when it comes to choosing between the men and the boys
    ah you great nipples of Babylon
                    Babies / you'll take the boys every time
            follow wide-eyed and terrified
                the howling crowds at rally
                    crowned with the long festoons of paper

                              falling from the frozen trees.

                    III

After the night of rally for the ball game
before the bulls rush each other across the frozen fields
while the thousands shout and the sparks of their breaths are wasted
upwards   upwards   upwards in an invisible fire
                    after a night of excrement and waste
I am full this morning of democratic vistas
enplaning at the southern fork of the coiling river
which ends by flowing North
                    through the golden womb of the Lady

          I am going away so as not to hear her
          not hear the seductions of her voice
          nor smell the rankness of her silences,
          strapped to my seat as the plane soars over the river
          I fail to hear the sirens' seductions
          gña yatter gña yatter gña yatter gña
          the mind prised loose from its sources
          the mouth telling lies by the skin of its teeth
          the terrible malformations of a language

Within her dome   covered with gold by the faithful
ah rich she was / yes wasn't she rich / not as if she weren't
                    like RICH I mean,
she tried to part, tried to open herself and tell me her secret
but there was room for *le sérieux* and all she could do was smile,
the priests had taught her the art of closure beyond all else
and she could never open again for another incarnation
but she said   and I take note of that statement for the future
while her virginity bled away like a sanctified heart


it is because you see of the pedestal, of the pedestal, of the pedestal. . .
     and I noticed true enough that she had been a statue



                    most of her golden life.


                                                            95

# SECTION: AMERICA (7): FROM THE POINT OF VIEW OF ANCHISES

" Denver, Colorado, 6 - 30 - 47,

And having once made up her mind
       that she was going to make me in her time
she the laughter-lover
       came to my hunting place in the mountains
and as she went
       she got together puma and ocelot, skunk and armadillo
and the great grizzly of Wyoming
       and the mountain cats of Oregon and Idaho
and they laughed when they saw her
       and went off into the woods to screw.

And 'You of this young City' she said
'You of this city destined to fame
but destined to fall in the end,
from the other side of the sea' she said
'I want your mortality.'
She stood. No, listen, it was as if a goddess.

I wasn't quite sure but addressed her respectfully from the start.
There was something very special about her.
The robe: maybe from Saks on Fifth,
the accessories: perhaps from Bloomingdales:
I'd seen all that back East a long time before when I was a kid.

No problem she told me: her father had oil in Texas
or was it copper in Bolivia or tin in the Argentine
or perhaps bananas in a number of Central American Republics:
it's tough to try remembering behind that experience.
The worst of it was, the jokes I mean.

She said 'I don't know anything about love,
I mean: I've never even necked in the back of a convertible —
why I can practically give you a certificate from the parish priest'
and all the time her nipples in that transparent dress
which as a matter of fact I couldn't really see through. . . .

It sounded like
       she was going to make an honest man of me
and give me a son
96

    for the sake of our City and our Constitution
and the moment I knew it was my luck
        to be the husband of such a girl
well I'd never fancied myself in the Cooper or Gable line
        but *there* was the evidence!
I told her I'd not let her go for a moment
        until we'd been to bed together she and I.

    And she LAUGHED and LAUGHED and LAUGHED
                            but in a shy way, you know.

I had a sort of den with mountain cat skins and laid her on those.

## II

And then I suppose I found myself making comparisons and computing
her age and the number of wrinkles that may have been beginning
to line her lovely face
                    and I
well I said to myself: 'This is by definition *perfect:* right?'
'O.K. if this is *perfect,* well what can I do for the rest of my life?'
'Well, if I've had *this,* what can I content myself with from now on?'
'I mean *creature features* ain't exactly going to keep me happy no more.'

I began thinking very hard about the exact shape of,
you know. . . her erogenous zones I guess you'd call them
I mean: stressing the bits of her so special that other men
would ask about them eventually, no matter how respectful,
(which is good reason why she said I should never say I'd laid her)
and I just. . .you know, wondered whether Sophie's in Chicago,
or that kid sister of the girl I'd been going with in Yokohama,
back in my Navy days and gotten such a shock from while sis was out —
well: if some of the things they had didn't compare favorably with. . .

what I'm groping for is, when you've had, you know, the very best,
I mean the finest barring none, the best product money can buy,
the product that's so good no ad can do justice to it,
the product any consumer report would say was indisputably tops,
when you've had that product even momentarily, even for a moment,
and enjoyed the experience to the full. . . what do you say?

    well what do you say?

WELL: WHAT DO YOU SAY?

Oh God to be the only man to sleep with Miss World before she married!
                                                                    97

## III

But the fact is that I remember not too much about it after all
except for her saying at some point
>> she'd bring back our kid when draft-aged.

She teased me awake after a while
>> and she stood at the door
of the hunting hut I'd built
>> and she was way taller than the door
which meant it was like her voice
>> was coming out of her navel
and I had to get up and look out the door
>> and up at her head in the clouds

She said: 'Do I look like I looked to you before?'
>> you know, all smart-like. . .

>> I had to admit she did not.

She said: 'Well if you ever tell my reputation has had it on Olympus.'
And I asked whether Olympus was in the Cascades or some place.
>> And she had to tell me not to be so dumb.

## IV

>> Oh Christ, all that perfection stuff.
I don't believe there's just one person in the world and all that.
>> I mean: is that what *you* believe?

>> Hey Charlie, please answer soon, O.K.?"


## SECTION: AMERICA (8): SHE TEARS HIM APART
>> AND SELLS HIM PIECEMEAL

On the sidewalks of Manhattan
>> the young go by at noon
>> as if they were going to live forever:
>> that throwaway gesture
>> >> those golden banners
>> >> they will lose by and by
>> their hands
>> >> closer and closer to their thighs.

The great white queens
            delicately setting tail to tarmac
                        their noses a little snotty in the air
        the long whine of their settling   their coming home
                        downed from the bright air of December
            into La Guardia / Newark / J.F.K.


Once in my life to achieve the physical perfection of woman
as it appears occasionally on the streets
a woman with no apparent blemish   no hidden blemish
as one said of life: to die and spend the rest of time regretting it
        but to have achieved it, once and for all,
        to have held it and be able to throw it away. . .


                sleek ships on the waves
                uptown / downtown the metal coffins
                        the metal rippling   the lap of waves
                Heraclitus looking down at the globe and weeping
                        flux of black steel and golden steel
                                in the melting streets


trying very hard to pretend
that the poem is compensation for perfection unfound
        the body unfucked and dry
but not succeeding and beauty intolerably hard to forgive:
                if the poem were to be remembered for ten years
                the stanza quoted for a hundred
                the line — ha! — for all eternity
STILL / there would be no forgiveness!


                and under the streets in the city's arteries
                the trains pulsing like poisons
                towards the Bronx / Brooklyn / Queens
                daughter of corn down there in her Gimbels dress
                & he with the dead in his palms looking across the aisle
                at the suburban bitches dissolving in their furs


*mais je n'veux pas tu sais qu'on parle de mon amour*
            you know: her name was X
        the name good god must have some resonance
something to last: Heloise, Francesca, Beatrice,
                        but what can you do with a name
            men joke about across the Fifty States?


                                                    99

I am not of a mind to be taken apart
I am not of a mind to be taken to pieces
I am not of a mind to be sold for scrap!

## II

Look I went to this god and said "Hey you: god of marriage
I think you're called and come to this wedding from the last one."
But he brought little luck and she tripped on a snake
and of course the snake bit her and took her down to the basement.
So I go down to this corngirl who's made it in the cellars meantime
and I say to her and her husband: "Look, I've tried very hard
but I can't live without my wife so I better have her back.
I mean: *you* know about love
                    you had a bit of it yourselves when you began.
And if I don't get her back I'll stay here, so."
Well I had some success with my speech because the rocks
the rocks were in tears and the ghosts and that poor bastard
forgot his water and the other one his stone
                    and those vultures laid off for a while
and it was the first time someone saw the three old girls crying.
        O.K. so they said, O.K.
Well I walked up again and kept my patience practically to the top
and then I thought jesus maybe the poor chick couldn't make it
you know in all that heat and cold alternating
so I looked back and she said nothing as she sank down again
I mean: you know she was very happy just that she'd been loved.

And somehow I couldn't make it with women from then on
and for three years I enjoyed screwing little boys
and they even pretend they hadn't heard of the custom there
                    the lying bastards!

## III

He is responsible to the world
                he has no time for you, just you.
He is responsible to the universe
                he cannot worry about a mere part of it.
Put too many women on the streets,
                too many beautiful people,
    and a kind of creeping impotence comes over him
and he cannot deal with one beautiful person,
                let alone the many.

He is very tired of these voices, by these voices,
                    he thinks these voices will make him mad.
    Some people call it the ten thousand things, the totality
and they advise getting away from it
                    in heart / navel / or scrotum.
From that privileged spot they say:
                    you will be able to deal with
and absorb the totality
                    and the totality will not destroy you.

He was sitting the story goes where the trees had grown round him
some spot in Central Park where fuzz and rapists let him be
but those goddam women came out of a meeting and found him
and he piped a whistle out of old habit and that got them mad
they picked up stones and sticks and flung them
but as long as he went on whistling the stuff let him be
but he got tired dodging it all and got hit more and more often
and the dead stuff grew crimson with his blood, it didn't hear.
Then they picked up railings and traffic signs
and they shot all that at his head and his last breath slipped away. . .

                              IV

Oh and it's said the birds fell out of the sky
and the rivers were swollen with tears and such stuff.

            and I was being sold for scrap all over town
            don't know what metal was fetching that particular day
            but the trade felt the pressure I can tell you.

She was taking me to pieces and looking hard inside
to find something she could use, something she could take back I guess
something she could put a name to, describe, identify,
when it came to keeping her records and compiling that dictionary.

            They're having a sale today on George Washington's birthday
            and on Lincoln's birthday too and on President Kennedy's
            and one in the middle of the George Washington Bridge
            and I guess in the Lincoln Tunnel too
            and perhaps in Reno and Las Vegas at the University of Nevada.

And I'm having the sale of my life with my wife underground
I got down there and found her and everything was the same again:
we loved again the orphan in each other

we stopped worrying about how we'd each die alone
because we'd died alone after all without stopping to think
because we'd always thought, and had no more thoughts to waste.

It's true we hadn't much above ground in the way of children
but you know all those dead seemed to need parents now
and turned to look at us with big goo-goo eyes
saying things like "Hey, I'm Jewish too"
or "you don't *have* to be, do you?"
and we'd say "no honey, no honey" soothingly
and "there, there, dinna worry, we're universal now"
and we told the revolution to fuck the revolution.

And I was dealing with so many things at my ease
you know, with my head breathing air and the real thing baby
and I wasn't pretending to make it in any academic setting
or pulling the scholarly woolbag over anyone's eyes
I even got angry some with all that crap about the birds crying
I mean jesus birds *crying*   all that anthropomorphic stuff
and said: look, cut this out of all trips to come
when you tell THIS story baby, make it for real, O.K.?

Wow that taking to pieces shit sure got me coming and going!

## SECTION: AMERICA (9): SHE IS THE MEMBERSHIP

To the peak of creation / inverted pit
the better to come down long day to evening,
    the sun   divided and eaten
        with a speck for the cardinal directions —
gone yet higher in contortions of rock
        so high to cloud-rock:
banks of green clover / plane of paradise

she trails behind so much herself.

Sun unwinds in the guts
the eyes open
and far more than the eyes:
look down and precision opens

102

look up, it is still far off
look down and precision opens
and the gates swing low and wide

They undoor the hinges of time:
ghosts at the edge of their eyes
                    ask
when was tomorrow?
They disarm the universal police,
they legislate at their sweet wills,
they are not hungry.

In the clover the nose knows
and the eyes aye
while the ears praise.
A butterfly with wings of grey marble
walks clover stalks with dancer's feet,
on the edge of his wings
two peacock's eyes
bulge from the diamond mosaic —
in every blade and stalk
the world's little lives have their bright day,
on the edge of vision-rims
the sky licks a tongue of blue

                    she sits alone and breathes so much herself.

## II

Bone man in his suit of bone,
he laughs down the canyon path as they go down,
he cannot stop laughing and asking
        why no one had told him it was so funny —
and half-Rome, dark Cicero, had said:
"it's funny it's holy it's everything,
but underneath it all is beauty"
        and Bone said: "You are very Navajo in spirit"
        and recited the Path of Beauty poem.
Virgil as *miles,* the other half of Empire,
handsome in curls, still blank about his function,
draped himself over rocks and dozed.

                    As they walked,
stopped, picked up stones, lay down,
opened jewelry shops on the canyon floors,
they gave themselves evening and morning among the stones
and the stones leapt like fleas in their hands.
        Now the whole shop was bathed in blood
and now the stones had the pallor of clover
and now her eyes darted out of the stones
in the fashion of mica or silver in rock —
        she toyed with the stones they gave her
        while they knelt at her feet
        and she so silent, and still so much herself.


Then he brought her down from the dead, winding down
the long day from creation, in the shapes of the Holy Women,
and there came a point when he looked forward instead of backward
for he thought to himself that the decision lay in him
not to look back at the followers (he knew no more than they did) —
and the Empire had told him that the Spirit after all
belonged to no one in this place in time, and now's astonishment
was all philosophers' by rights, and also all the clowns'
        — he took the shard she had handed him
        saying: "this'll be for your rice and beans"
        and, grasping the bone he had found among clovers,
        he went on down, not looking back


but thought:
        and yet:   *must* have looked back many a time
                                *in that dire poverty?*

                            III

        Time of day, waiting, lying still, face in clouds,
        face in water clouds, hand inside
        mirrors of water, head in a rock-cleft,
        laughter in grass, smile in the slanting sun


and the gladiator lying back, throat exposed
while she took his spark from the jugular,
and the dark clown sitting hunched
hands around knees — she took his spark from his eyes,
and the man of bone, standing in motherwater,
she took his spark from his two ankles,
half the spark in the one, half in the other.

104

She sat in the lotus posture down by the river
while all the religions whispered round her head,
her face bent to the ground of the canyon —
now drinks the distillation of her own sparks through the nose,
head thrown back in an attitude of supplication.

    There'll be no coming back this time round
    there's no more to take in   nowhere we haven't been
    everything is beauty and love and so laughter
    everything is the beauty compounded daily.

IV

When he brought her down from the dead, canto unnumbered,
explaining that he had been into Tuscan studies for some time
                        and so could bore,
    (but everything was permitted to the divine child)
they arrived at the dividing river
   and the two halves of Empire melted into each other
as they climbed up and down the rocks,
      — but when the time came that they should part
and the Empire melt back into the soil of New Mexico,
   they did not depart
      nor were they lost, nor did they melt into
                      the INSUBSTANTIAL AIR. . .

The earth was writhing in fire,
the vast spine of earth lunged into the sky,
   head thrown back in an attitude of supplication,
it was all he could do not to throw himself at earth's feet
    far down where the people were laughing on their picnics
    and throwing beer cans at each other
                 liquor of lost and found.

    They had been tracked, and were awaited
    by those on the other side of the river:
                 the family reunited
   with shouts of soldiers having found the sea
   and she said he deserved a wreath of laurel
   for the nose for the classics he was gifted with,
   and without a single movement of her hands
   nor being seen by anyone of the family present,
   she wove the wreath of laurel and clover
   and placed it on his brow.

(and the canyon-spirit arrived
        but split three ways:
    one with beer can, one with transistor,
    third goating it from bush to bush
    three Nambe men wagging fat fingers,
        gone quickly round a rock)

V

In the cool night the membership lay down
waiting for a new sun

        And the bitter judgment of loud music
        bathed the last day on earth.


## SECTION: AMERICA (10): MESCALITO AS LAZULI


The head of the bird which went in front of them,
like an annunciation, was of turquoise in the sun,
the back of turquoise also, catching the rays slanting,
blood-wash on breast, and on the wings, a white bar
(mantle of angels, weighted down, hunched on a distant fence)
        —and the head opened:
inside it a world was born, twined with old man's beard,
sweet clematis and sage in the path of the visiting wind
walking in fragrance of welcome towards these pilgrims.

Tree branches like tentacles
groping for sky like an octopus under water,
the whole earth breathing, their shoes breathing
discarded on the grass, their clothes breathing
discarded on the grass, and they disposing their clothes
on the brainlines of the lazuli — the crimson veins
opening out and breathing and closing again
pulsing with earth around them and with grass,
each blade of grass dilated, shrunk, dilated, shrunk

Hours growing to moments, moments shrinking to hours,
        all day they gave birth to each other,
slipping in and out of each other,
        bodies breathing as if lungs —
he said how can a man be a father who is about to be born

she laughed as she bore him in and out of herself
while she turned to child in the grass, and to mother,
and also to old woman,
                    and all the stages in between.

He looked into her thigh as she turned,
uncreased one of the stretch marks on her skin
and fell into an ocean out of which he was born
            yet again in a tangle of spiders,
there was nothing but peace, except for the noise of flies,
they lay exposed for all to see had anyone strayed
under a sun which could not be told from ice,
and whether the sun was consuming them or freezing them
it was impossible to tell    in that radiance

Buffalo Bill and old Larrom of Valley
stood at the doors of the State of Wyoming
holding banners of all the many times Fifty States
bright with a thousand emblems, bars and stars
and all the heraldry of both their lives:
it was like an indigo sky at night, star-studded,
and the gates were opening out while they planted the race
leading into the Ideal Republic of Pacific America
the very furthest far western West that anyone could conceive

But when he stood up at last, circling the garden
throwing ashes of food before and behind
above and below and in the middle
clothed only in a necklace of silver,
and she lay still curved in the foetal position
shaped by his arms in the smithy of love,
the patch of earth they had fallen into
burned with well-being and came to be called Eden
came to be called *Paradiso Terrestre* after those who had gone before.

        The bird had gone
but they talked freely to the spirits and the spirits heard:
whatever the place was named, it came to be called *Matrimony*
and *Generation,* whether there'd been children or not,
            as the old bush he'd once been
burned with Israel's loss and the borning of a New World
            and they went out to eat and drink the river.
        They collected each other throughout the day
but for long after, when they'd turned back in time,

107

the bodies of their minds lay there in Eden grass
        covered with spiders and flies,
        the bodies lay there abandoned,
the bodies remained there where they had planted the race.
The bodies, in a sense, would always be lying there:
the imprint in their minds of the bodies lying there in the grass,
        at the making of Eden surrounded with trees,
the whole surrounded with hills and embedded in night's feathers,
        and the planet turning round, and they at rest.


## SECTION: AMERICA (11): AT GLOUCESTER, MASS., AFTER FOREIGN TRAVEL

At Gloucester, Mass., after foreign travel,
    Labor Day mists
            the lovely breath of one more Summer dying out,
the sea
            swelled contrapuntally as we swam
and a smell of old furniture came up from the water
                        into the dusting sunlight. . .


As if all the woods that had gone down into the sea
                        surfaced to farewell Summer
the boats crossed and crisscrossed over the drowned
                        and the great feast of work
crimson with lobster shells, stubbed toes and girls' bandannas
                        set round the pink of nipples
in loose red shirts / O flag of love over America the damned!


We went down to the sea
all the poets together
and gave ourselves up to the waters
                        in various positions of loss:
I realized that I had never died into water
                        and within five minutes
after giving myself completely to the wave

                        I did about ten things
never done in my life before
such as: throwing my body like a javelin into the waves
spreading myself like a banner on the swell
somersaulting in the deep

holding the sand's thighs in my hands
                              and all the fear was gone —

We had spent the whole day looking for loons and grasses
old Dogtown had risen for us from the ground
and Charles Olson's floor and windowboards full of dates
had defied the policy on National Monuments —
        white building slats among the red stripes
                              the stars on my Union Jack
exclusive to the night:


                              and she seen rightly
had no need to be touched
                              she seen rightly
became a thousand faces one after another
                              seen rightly
there was no face the world could take on which was not her face
                              and a golden aura

red with cheap scents raved round her hair.
                        Oh the hands that went out,
the bodies that moved out towards her on our belief,
                        Labor Day, Gloucester, Mass.,
the copulations that sped towards her on the arrow of sight
                        drawing no flesh at all
out of its sheathing!

                        The America he dreamed never existed,
                        cause of lost causes —
                        but dreamed it with the throat of need
                        the passionate thirst of a tramp
                        sweat on his whiskers.
                        And she in whose hands lies my life
                        brings her creased eyes to town

brings her body like a banner
she said she could not use
        advertising ships, and land, and whispers among hutments,
and "today," she said, "today,"
    "tears of blood coming out of the ground
at what has become of this Republic
                        which was to be the laughter of the world!"

If it be true / that this polity
has killed Allende for instance / has killed Neruda
if it be true that Spain is being repeated — billed to this polity —
                    then the devices of the world of ice
the hanging in the maws of the old windmill the great Giver devised
                    shall be but as childsplay to what awaits
our shabby emperor in his greasy feathers -/-/-

                *encore une fois l'refrain*

        Swallow on the air
        mackerel in the sky
        mackerel in the water
        swallows on the sea
                    stitching silver to silver
        in the heart's water:
                        I am so glad to be home!

                    I have laid up a world of words
for the immortal gods of this Republic
that all the 50 stars might sing in unison together!
                    Our moods of love
as they will seize and shake us all our lives:
wood rising from the sea, trees soaring on first shores,

            the Adam-hut, its ghost,

                        I am so glad to be home!

## SECTION: LA TRAVIATA (1): BEFORE KNOWING HER


The morning, fresh with spring boughs,
their muslin round her form already as she emerges
from pigsty to the streets, her clogs ringing,
smudges of ash on her cheek.

When everyone had ceased to hope, when no object of possible belief
existed any longer, when all cards had been stacked on love's behalf
against the looming dark — she brought her faultless taste to town,
her fragrant curls into the tapestry.

First: a child of the wild wood. Then a peasant, to the Capital.
Then, picked up by so and so, Montmorency. Then settled in rooms.
The jacob's-ladder of her fame: opera, balls, Tortoni's,
on the arm of this or that frock-coat of green moiré.

She had the hush of death in her perfect mouth, her teeth
framed the throat of consumption, her skin ran with blue veins,
she leant against fireplaces mildly, she strangled in asides,
men saw their own *ennui* perfectly reflected in her pallor.

And taken at last, after death, by the wings of an imagination.
Not a great one, but a popular one, with a thousand avid hearers
bringing her favorite flower on stage as to a wedding.
The cortege-followers sitting in subscribed stalls.

Made poetry, with an aside here and there, by one imagination:
This is what I had of her, a great love it was, after the fashion —
Chateaubriand, Byron, Hugo, the Sage of Weimar suffered for this:
sighed for this love to be placed on the boards and worshipped.

Her insignificance. What is this story, after all, this life
of a courtesan of Paris in the days of the great *heterae* —
their names a Homeric list to be appended hereafter —
asides the author cannot verify tortured in the French prose,

the sentence wandering as the spider wanders over silk walls,
under the bed where her lovers lie altogether in their death,
moaning with her moan and coughing out their lungs,
where she gives them back their splendor in the moment of dying?

111

Abandoned by the regents of this life,
by the frail queens in their humid bodies, I ask
      of the dead what part of history they own
what they can bring me in this night of spiders,

      (Though there had been a body recently,
middling between those I have known / splendid in walk at night,
naked from bed, long, slender, to the windowframe,
door, and beyond, leaving a wake of perfumes. . .

      but she has gone to Kalifornia
to fornicate with another, whom she does not love.
      In the humid Eastern dusk
I am left with spiders on the wall, and spiders in the mind.)

A government as sinister as any known to men
staining all stretches of these States. At night, the spiders
move on the gloss of my mind towards perfection. Her scent
of love among my fingers, short hairs among my fingers.

We shall ask of wisdom, simply, what it still has to offer,
we shall ask in this watershed what minds remain,
what conversation is extant to bring mind and mind together
      to justify communion of the body.

      The Second Empire sourcebooks say
those thirty years were the years of confessional writing,
perfect accord of life and art, courtesy of avowal
      never known since as fine:

      A lover's gift to the reading eye
of a public too eager to give itself in return.
Eylau and Austerlitz consumed, the flags a memory.
      Waterloo of arms and spirit.

### III

Before knowing her, I know her perfections arose
more beautifully in those days than any since out of a boil of lace,
the contrast being between flesh revealed and flesh covered —
sylph-like neck, heave of cameoed breast, juncture of arm

and breast, where ringlets fall, just grazing the shoulders.
Music begins. Various degrees of commitment to this image:
various artists' say: changing her name, romanticizing her,
layer on layer of persona over the gathering legend.

The masks of the powerful over the skull.
All government, plunging towards Empire again denatured, officials
sick of a sickness in the air, a gathering loudness of moneys,
        bloat purse of time / and the people thwarted,

the body politic apologizing to the father of the people
*Dite a la giovinne si bella e pura:* O Young America
how lost you are among your provinces, your one glazed eye
        stripping the secrets of your fathers' sins!

and her eyes in a smile of compassion,
so pardoning among her luxuries, her loveliness so piteous,
*excusez-moi d'être ainsi parmi vous, sans être à la hauteur*
        I that am bought with fortunes, lost with them:

                    spider in iron web.


## SECTION: LA TRAVIATA (2): MY RIVER IN THE DARK


Her voices, in a Paradise of first flowers,
            each one a return to our earliest memories,
when she said "Go in peace, John, and in my protection,
            this confederacy your servant unto the Alleghenies,
go in the warmth of the polity, Sebastian,
            these tribes your warrant unto the Adirondacks,
Go in the pipesmoke of brotherhood, Martin,
            unto the desert mountains and Quebec."

My river flows in the dark tonight, welcoming home.
The history of my passions, great tree out of the river,
the waters curving round its trunk towards the sea.
Roots: each one a cathedral buttress, joining the trunk
high in the air where her mouth presses against the dark,
the trunk itself gnarled with years, the boles: children.
Each one with a tree of his own in the surrounding streams.
And soaring into the branches, all the arms of my pleading,

all my desire white-fanged: the forms emprisoned there
within the body of the tree / into the leaves,
colossal umbrage over the river, traversed by swallows,
martins and swifts of Summer, tearing the air
                              as if with witch claws —

I caught her footsteps in the dark, walking up and down,
felt her tread in the carpet of leaves,
        she declared herself a wise virgin, read in much lore,
though innocent of love.
        I knew her profile that I had never seen in this life,
being a child in her splendid days, as she served tea in London,
waiting for the walls to close in.
        And of a woman so much older, so much unmet down here,
can it be predicated: the thigh's lining, that secret humor,
the dark hair — a choice of dark or blonde, but dark I imagine,
        and of the exact length of the hair,
                UP, UP, to the PROFILE: in the photos, dead *many*
years, and the lighthouse over the James River. . . ?

Back of that, the mothers of the divine conglomerate,
black-skirted, cowled like nuns, elegant,
their voices whining to puppies in a foreign accent,
among them one adolescent whose blood was to be mine,
past river of becoming, risen out of corsage,
first-morning-flower, serious lips above a set of chin,
severe, nose of young eagle, eyes under brow, severe,
middle parting of hair, severe / but, overall,
a softness like that of creation before it had memorized the rosters.
White correspondences of dresses, Sundays, in Paris,
in the Bois de Boulogne, with the phaetons passing,
broad alleys greened with lawns at the margins, picnic tables,
white cloths and white porcelain, set for *le five o'clock.*

She lies underneath me, flesh welcoming as a bed after travels.
I sleep in her hollows and dream in each of her valleys another dream.
Waking, I open her doors, into deeper dreams with no beginning.
(Paint me your eros, he had said: submit your archetypes.)
Of a sudden: she: bone, white, unyielding. Into my ear on the left,
little finger exploring, her chin into my throat, knuckles
inside my sockets. The cushions deflate: I fall into bone pits.
The shank is thin like a flute, but without music — the elbow
digs into my ribs. A shudder wrenches cock and balls.
                              Disembowelment.

114

She was flying over Chikago away from me into Kalifornia and already
she was writing to say she missed me out of our dark, and would return,
after savoring, of course, what Kalifornia had to offer, but it seemed
to me/she was so far/ so far/it was unspeakable how far/
and I felt dull with the dullness of several centuries between us
as if I had never met this incarnation of her.
And, as for me, I was working my way through the historical stacks,
State by State in alphabetical order, now close, now far,
and the polity was sinking under history for the first time totally,
the headman pathetic in his fineries exposed for what they were.


## SECTION: LA TRAVIATA (3): AMERICAN FRAMEWORK


He had come    from the Summer Islands, originally,
         the sun    had charred his blood — and his complexion
was more than tan. He could have gone back there
         when she told him,
              when she let him know no single love could dry
the rain of coin she lived on daily.
         There was still time to make fortunes
instead of whiling away his Morocco. . .

    It could have been:
    "Tell them,
    tell them we are engaged / tell them
    we are about to marry
         our younger sister of Amerika:
    there will be no break.
         The continuity will be assured
    and the succession in case of children.
         We shall not forget one jot of home,
    it will be merely: a convenience
         as all these unions have been    outside of love,
    a way
         of getting about the land
                             without embarrassment."


She is of similar physique
she is almost the merger one dreams of
         between one beloved and another
when a man
         desperate to put together his shadows

wishes they'd blend in the flesh —
and of somewhat the same fortune:
                                    at ease in her furnishings,
strongly reminiscent
        of all he had learned to enjoy.
She has parents, in the wings, easy-going,
        well-wishing, bestowing land and houses,
estates where the Cadillacs ply
                        with ravenous guests.

## II

"I have begun the novel I told you about.
By the way: if by any chance you have kept the letters
        I sent you since my departure,
do me the favor of bringing them back." (Musset to Sand).
*"La maladie du siècle"*(Musset).*"La maladie de René"*(Sainte-Beuve).
        "I have been bored all my life."(Byron).
"My youth dipped me into I know not what opium of boredom
        for the rest of my days" (Flaubert to Maxime du Camp).

"A state of great bitterness,
proceeding from young, active, full faculties,
when they exercise but on themselves: no goal, no object."
(Chateaubriand) Who yawned the length of his life.
"In the age of energetic passions, we no longer have passions,
if it be not to make an end of fatigue, and rest as in a coffin" (Sand).
Shut in a high, proud desolation. Derval, then cancer. (de Vigny).

And woman:
"She was thirsty for what was not the clear water of her life,
        hidden among the grasses." (Balzac).
A whore to Maxime du Camp: "I would so much like that for myself,
a man who would be pale and serious." / She came through the forest,
        warning me that the King had planned a raid
upon the settlement
        and when I pressed upon her
jewels and beads
        she said she could not take back any bestowals,
for fear the King would know she had had commerce with me.
Eight years later, in London, she to my younger brother
        joined in sweet marriage,
I, father to the plantations, who have no wife, no children,
        praised her to the reigning Queen.

# III

In the land where everything has turned to heart,
        where intellect
is suspect to the workings of the individual conscience, God-prodded,
        she has, oh contrast!, always hated her flesh.
I am of no use to anyone, to any *man*, if he have not my body,
        this loathsome thing,
that I cannot enjoy with any *man* I love,
        but give away to the forest beast,

                                    the fox-colored rapist,

        to feel my pit sing.
— Dear sweet bone, slender and comfortable, smooth to touch,
        it has been warm with you
and I have recognized our large new Kingdome of Virginitie
        in these locked timbers.

                        American woman: your shattered gateways!


## SECTION: LA TRAVIATA (4): WOMAN'S EXPENSIVE,
##                          ART'S PRICES FOLLOW

*Alexandre Dumas Fils to Sarah Bernhardt:*

"My Dear Sarah,
Allow me to offer you a copy of *La Dame aux Camélias*
                which has become rare.
What makes this copy unique is the *als.* you will find
                inserted at the 212th page
which is very close to the letter in the printed text at that point.
                This letter was written
by the real Armand Duval some forty years ago
                : it doesn't make him any younger.
His age was your own son's today.
                The letter turns out to be
THE ONLY PALPABLE THING to have survived that story.
                You own it as of right
since it is you who have just resurrected the dead past.
                Keep it in any case
as a souvenir of the lovely evening, last Saturday
                and as an unworthy keepsake

117

of my very great admiration and warmest gratitude.

With this,

I applaud you with all my strength and embrace you
with all my heart. A.D. 1/28/1884.''

*Alexandre Dumas Fils to Marie Duplessis:*

'' My Dear Marie,
I am not rich enough to love you as I would wish,
nor poor enough to be loved as YOU would desire it.
Let's both of us forget:

a name which must, by now, be quite indifferent to you,
a happiness for me become impossible.
No use telling you my sadness,

since you already know how much I love you.
Farewell.

You have too much heart to misunderstand the causes of my letter,
too great a mind not to forgive it me. A thousand memories.
A.D. 8/30/1845.''

*Marguerite Gautier to Armand Duval:*

'' When you will read this note, Armand, I will already be
another's mistress. We're through.
Go back to your father my friend, *dite a la giovinne, si bella e pura,*
— your sister chaste, our misery unknown —
at whose side you will soon forget what this lost Marguerite
you loved a moment will have made you suffer,
who owes you the few happy moments of a life she hopes ends soon.
Marguerite Gautier.''

*To Marie Duplessis, alias Marguerite Gautier, alias Violetta Valery:*

"Madam:

Anxious to redeem an adolescence distinguished by no romantic adventures, I beg the honor to be received into your bed — there to enjoy the favors so inordinately praised by those fortunate enough to have been your contemporaries. It is said of you, despite the great care you have of adorning your beauty, and of administering to it with all the resources at your lovers' commands, that you are a woman of heart and wit, rather than a plaything of riches. I am a poet, born of the underworld, now come to rest in a small corner of Pennsylvania in the United States. My youth was spent in dreams of unachievable love. Above all, I have always regretted not being born in the time of phaetons and silver clouds, white picnics in cool parks, and all the refinements of music and dance I associate with the waltz. It is not so much that I have been unloved by women — or even that I have not enjoyed the favors of a great courtesan — but rather that, like men of my temperament born under any clime, I have rarely exhausted my passions in the one and only, but have always run after the many in a desperate attempt to make time stop.

O Violetta, Marguerite, Marie, Alphonsine,
                              by whatever name they call you,
I learn that, when Alexander met you in his troubled search,
the camellia you wore at your breast was still tinged with red.
Wherefore you told him to return it when it would have faded —
or, in my reading, when it would have become again white.
Know of my intimacy that I am so kindred to the blood of woman
that the great meetings of my life have taken place under its sign.
Welcome me back then, to where there are no fathers and mothers,
take me to the altar of your body in the keep of perfect time,
and, since you cannot hack the scent of any other flower, believe me

Always yours in a perfumeless time. Nathaniel Tarn. 6/9/1973."


## SECTION: LA TRAVIATA (5): FATHERS AND SONS


"Follow me to the *Théâtre Français*.
Box-door opens. Stopped by my frock-coat.
I turn: Alexander, my son, detains me.
Close eyes. Pop head through door. He reassures me.
Indeed, no sooner eyes closed, I feel on my lips
the pressure of shivering lips (her mark), feverish, burning.
Open eyes: adorable young woman, 20-22, *en tête à tête*
                              with Alexander.
Recognize her from several visits to the *Théâtre*:
                              Marie Duplessis."


"I, Alexandre Dumas, Père: You, beautiful child?
Marie: Yes. You have to be raped it seems?
I: Say that aloud! They may believe you!

M: Oh I know very well that's not your reputation!
But then, why *are* you so cruel to me?
Twice I've invited you to the *Opéra* Ball.

I: In front of the clock, at two a.m.?

M: You see! you *did* receive my letters!

I: Perhaps.

M: Then why didn't you come?

I: Because from one to two in the morning, in front of the clock,
only wits of 20-30, or older imbeciles, disport themselves.
As I'm fully forty, I would be classified among the imbeciles
by objective observers. I do not choose to be humiliated.

M: I fail to understand.

I: A girl like you only calls men of my age
when she needs something from them.
What can I do for you? I am at your disposal,
I offer you protection, and you need not fake love.

M: Ah (she sd., with a charming smile,
veiling her eyes with long, black lashes,)
then we shall go to see each other some time, Sir, shall we not?"


(Sir. Darling. I am a student, and you are a professor.
I am tired of the ignorance of my peers of the male gender
and would like to use my option of taking an older lover.
You will teach me everything you have learned, in your long travels,
in your exhaustive readings and your experiences of womankind.
I will begin by telling you my life: birth (my), parentage (my),
schooling (my), college days (my), young lovers (my), sex experience (my),
difficulties in achieving orgasm. I know you will sit there,
wondering whether you will ever get a word in edgeways,
and I shall be distressed, thinking that I may bore you and impose.
Yet my tongue runs away with me, and my desire
to drag you into my world and wrap you tight in its web
until you are unable to remember a single one of your thoughts.
Then, hopefully, you will write poems for me of inexpressible grandeur.)


My father, methinks I see my father!
                                        — Where, my Lord?
In my mind's eye, gay blade in his young twenties,
thinking himself the heir to Shakespeare in our garret,
throws me across the room in a fit of temper,
throws me to college like a dog to kennels —
                    years of harrowing exile, (my mother dying,
love will not tarnish for her destroyer.)

Later, rid of permanent women, drowned into work,
to replenish the cup others will drain from nightly,
reaches the night, 44, with a son he is proud of, 22:
they boulevard together: an idyll.
Sequences of lovers, astonishing: appetites for work and sex
as large as each other. This society
knows itself well. I could spend a lifetime, in wonderment,
collating the meetings, moment by moment, hour by hour, day by day.
A calling on B. B dining with C. C fucking D. And round the circle.
Women at home, and women of the world, have the same thoughts,
same dresses, same preferments, same reading lists.
The energy of these people! The forty volume *oeuvres*,
giants in appetite and in achievement. And still the time
to knot sargassoes nightly between sheets!

## II

Though living at home, and available, theoretically, every moment,
a father can abandon his son. A father can omit to praise his son,
though he speak well of him to everyone behind his son's back.
Thus the work that the son does goes into a bottomless vase.
The son acquires no knowledge of fatherhood, moves ignorant
as an untrained animal into his own conceptions. His own son
will gift him the bird of his soul, and he will smother it,
delay the feeding of the bird until the bird dies,
clawing at the mixture of sand and seed that carpets his cage.
Or the son will appear to the inner father in his dreams,
sprouting up like a mushroom from under a table, at a gathering,
and they will have a good time together, the inner father
stifling his tears of recognition, unable to see his own shadow.
Thus the sins of the fathers, visited on several generations.

I have given away my own children, like a cannibal to an overlord.

Since you were never able to be my father, I'll go into exile
and there build the only manhood I can achieve, far from your house.
And I'll say to you: Marry my wife / take her as your wife or your child,
no matter, and take the offspring of my loins as your children also.
Pay them and keep them alive with the moneys you have saved for me
and let me use the moneys I have earned with the sweat of *my* brow
for the erection of *my* own house. And I shall look for,
in the love of very young women, whose lips mix my seed
with their mothers' milk scarcely dry on their lips, my own land,
I shall build up my own colonies, with their own products and crafts:

121

"those children: for they have been my wife, my hawks, my hounds, my cards, my dice, and, in total, my best content," *and*
"Those countries I ofttimes used to call my children, and well I might, for few fathers ever paid dearer for so little content."

"They had heard that we were people come from under the world
TO TAKE THEIR OWN WORLD FROM THEM."


## SECTION: LA TRAVIATA (6): THE WAGES


"A lot of them wondered — they want to take you out to dinner, want to talk to you; they want to mimic the behavior of lovers. Maybe that's what they want. Some of them really do want that — to be lovers. They fall in love with you. That's very hard to take. I never liked that. Because that was crossing the boundary — it wasn't business anymore. And this was business: it wasn't love."

"And the old line about 'How could a nice girl like you get into a business like this?' That's really said a lot. It's said a lot, especially by people who seem educated or middle class. And then sometimes they tell you that you aren't really a whore. I had a guy who I was seeing — about a month ago — I actually couldn't take it any longer. He gave me a lot of money. He was a very, very old guy — about sixty-seven. He was in love with me, and he would keep telling me, 'You're not a whore.' He was so hung up. Poor man. You have to feel sorry for someone who's that screwed up. And the guys who want you to quit, they want you to be true, like they feel you're cheating if you're whoring. Very few men will understand that when a woman screws for money, she has no involvement at all. Yet *they* can just go out and get laid and feel no involvement. And the guy who wants you to quit: he's seeing you as property; he's changing you, from like currency, which passes from hand to hand, to something like real estate. *Real* property. There's an *owning* thing about wanting you to quit, especially if the guy is poor."

"The undersigned physicians opine that Mme. Duplessis:

i)     shall have the armpits frictioned every night with a hazel nut's size's worth of potassium iodide cream at 1/10th.

ii)    shall continue to take her usual potions, alternating with a solution of *ficus crispus*.

iii)     shall return to she-ass milk, sweetened with syrup of maidenhair fern *(adiantum)*.

iv)     shall have, to aid sleep at night, a mixture of equal parts of sweet almond milk and bitter almond milk (60 grs. each); 2-5 grs. of thebaic extract (Egyptian opium) to be added progressively.

v)      shall moderate perspiration with a teaspoon of 1-2 grs. of soft extract of quinquina, wrapped in altar bread, to be taken daily with the first spoonful of soup.

vi)     the diet shall be composed of soup or rice bouillon, fresh eggs: boiled or scrambled; light fish, grilled or in wine sauce; fowl; vegetables boiled in bouillon; well-risen bread, stale and canary bread; fruit compote; jam; hot chocolate for breakfast. At meals: *Eau de Bussang* cut with 1/6th of wine.

vii)    shall take walks whenever the weather permits between noon and 3 p.m. Shall not leave the house morning or evening until further notice.

viii)   shall sleep on horsehair rather than wool.

ix)     shall speak little, and never loudly.

Davaine, Chomel. 9/11/1846."

"After that I didn't walk the streets anymore because I was still getting referrals from an employment agency dealing in waiters, cooks and things like that. I went down there one day to get a job. I was going to get a job before Saturday and this was a Friday afternoon. So there weren't any jobs and I was just hanging around. I ran into a guy there who was also looking for a job. He was trying to pick me up. It was a wild thing: I ended up going over to Brooklyn. He didn't want to buy me. I got scared he was a cop or something. He was pretty nice: a black guy. He wanted to set up a thing where he'd see me every week and go twice — for twelve fifty. And he wanted to pay my rent. Going twice — that means he screws me twice. It's a very bad deal because they take forever going the second time. That going twice business, I got out of that."

"The undersigned physicians opine that Mme. Duplessis:

i)      shall take daily an enema prepared with a solution of starch in which 30 grs. of quinine sulfate will be dissolved with the aid of a little vinegar. To be held as long as possible.

ii)     shall replace the decoction of *ficus crispus* with coltsfoot syrup, sweetened with marshmallow syrup.

iii)    shall take in the evening, against the cough, 10 grs. of yellow amber syrup, repeatable if necessary.

iv)    in case of frequent coughing, shall use fumigations of poppy flower infusions.

v)     shall sustain her energies with easily digestible but substantial foods.

vi)    shall continue the use of she-ass milk, diluted with Tolu syrup, *(myrospermum toluiferum)*; also the *Eau de Bussang*.

Davaine, Chomel. 9/13/1846."

"I would so much rather turn a trick with somebody than go out on a date. Turning a trick is not anxiety-producing. But going out on a date, I just freak out. Of course, on a date you may kid yourself that it's your personality they like. But when you're whoring, it's sometimes your personality they like too. There's one guy who comes to the studio regularly, he does other things with other people, but he gives me ten dollars just to talk to me. For shrinking too, you get ten dollars while they talk. And that's why I think I'm going into it. When I was in therapy I saw such parallels between the two things — prostitution and psychiatry — kinds of therapy. And then all the money they make. Like, I thought, here's a way I can legitimately do all this. I felt always that my analyst was doing the same thing I'd been doing, but respectably. After all I was in prostitution before I got into therapy. In fact I couldn't afford analysis until I was a prostitute. And therapy is what got me back into school, graduate school, and out of prostitution."

*RAGONOT, 14 Rue de la Paix, Florist (One, among many)*    *Statement*

|  |  | francs |
|---|---|---|
| . . . . . . . . | | |
| 11/9/1843 | Sold to Mme. Dupleci (sic) to date. . . . . . | 3 |
| | 9 pots of flowers . . . . . . . . . . . . . . . . | 15 |
| 11/16 | 2 sprays of (illegible). . . . . . . . . . . . . | 6 |
| 11/23 | 4 camellia, set and mounted . . . . . . . . . | 12 |
| 11/30 | 2 sprays of camellia . . . . . . . . . . . . . . | 6 |

| | | |
|---|---|---:|
| 12/23 | 2 white camellias, s.m. . . . . . . . . . . . . | 5 |
| 1/2/1844 | 1 Hand bouquet. . . . . . . . . . . . . . . . . | 15 |
| | 1 camellia, imperialist . . . . . . . . . . . . . | 3 |
| 5/2 | 2 camellia, s.m. . . . . . . . . . . . . . . . . | 4 |
| 8/2 | 1 Hand bouquet; 4 camellias, s.m. . . . . . . | 20 |
| 11/2 | 5 azaleat (sic) . . . . . . . . . . . . . . . . . . | 15 |
| 12/2 | 2 Roses du Roy . . . . . . . . . . . . . . . . . | 16 |
| 12/2 | 1 heather . . . . . . . . . . . . . . . . . . . . . | 3 |
| 12/2 | 1 pot of Holland Hyacinth . . . . . . . . . . . | 2 |
| 14/2 | 1 Hand Bouquet. . . . . . . . . . . . . . . . . | 20 |
| | 2 sprays of camellia . . . . . . . . . . . . . . | 8 |
| | 9 pots of Holland Hyacinth . . . . . . . . . . | 16 |

|  |  |
|---|---:|
| | 184 |
| Credit: | 20 |
| Total due: | 164 |

"The undersigned physicians counsel the following measures:

i)   Use Swiss Alpine flower tea as an infusion (falltrank): continue use of quinine enemas and yellow amber.

ii)  use Iceland moss.

iii) continue same diet and hygienic precautions.

Davaine, Chomel. 9/10/1846."

"The cops delicately refer to the vice squad, the plain clothes unit that does all the prostitution arrests, as the Pussy Brigade. And that's just the way they see it; it's just picking up the cunt, bringing it in, and letting it go loose again. Obviously there's a lot of graft going on, a lot of give and take between the women and the cops; they've known each other for a long time and they're known to watch out for each other."

"The scene in court is astonishing: the woman is absolutely flirting throughout the whole proceedings. She's doing it when she comes in; she does it when she goes out with the cops and clerks. It doesn't break down for a minute. That interchange is very weird to watch, and it's something that would take a long time to explain, but you know the woman's security and advantage lies in maintaining this relationship."

Dr. Koreff, to whom she owes 1400 frs. & who had been giving her 1 cgr. of strychnine per day, voided

Dr. Manec, of *La Salpétrière:* 39 visits (9/18 — 11/19/1846)

Dr. Chomel, physician in ordinary to His Majesty)
Dr. Louis, professor at the *Hotel-Dieu*   ) special consultations.

Dr. Davaine, from 5/1846 on:

| | | |
|---|---|---|
| 9/46: | 3 visits | 11 bandages for an abcess. |
| 10/46: | 37 visits | 4 consultations w. Chomel. |
| 11/46: | 44 visits | 3 consultations w. Louis. |
| 12/46: | 35 visits | |
| 1/47: | 39 visits | ———————————— |
| 2/47: | 8 visits | 184 visits: 1.025 frs. |

*DEATH OF MARIE DUPLESSIS: EARLY HOURS OF 2/3/1847:*

having received absolution of a priest,
*"jambon pour le praître (sic): 2 frs."* –Clotilde's journal.

flannel waistcoat rushed by de Perrégaux to Alexis Didier,
              somnambulist in the fashion:
"Go back at once she has few hours to live". . .

and held three whole days Clotilde's hand, her servant, giving her instructions to delay the funeral as much as possible and, above all,
              to install a little bolt on the coffin for: "I have always had the idea one might come back to life"
and at the end:
"stood bolt upright, cried out 3 times, fell back lifeless."
              Gautier: *Le Pays,* 3/9/1852.

Apocryphal Report, *l'Opinion Nationale,* 4/24/1868: "As she needed the rough smell of the stable for her lungs, an elegant boudoir had been set up for the dying woman near the *barrière Fontainebleau,* the floors of which had holes in it, above the sleeping quarters of a milkman's cows. Downstairs: the cow-shed. Upstairs: the tapestries, silk hangings, chinoiseries and bronzes."

"For the prostitute, probably the ultimate oppression is the social onus with which she is cursed for accepting the agreed-upon social definition of her femaleness, her sexual abjectification. A Marxist analysis here is quite inadequate, as it fails to take psychological factors such as shame into account. For there is a crucial element quite beyond the economic. Perhaps it might be described as a kind of psychological addiction, to self-denigration, an addiction I feel all women are socially conditioned to accept. In a sexual culture as unhealthy as our own, it is reiterated again and again through the manner of our sexual acts that the female is carnality — cunt. It is as though cunt were posed as the opposite of ego or selfhood, its very antithesis, the negative pole of selfhood or spirit. The sale of women in prostitution reinforces this attitude more powerfully than any other event."

"Seeing it all, a strange perception came over me. That prostitutes are our political prisoners — in jail for cunt. Jailed for it, for cunt, the offense we all commit in just being female. That's sexual politics, the stone core of it."

*CALENDAR:*

Sunday, 12/6/1846: *La Damnation de Faust,* Hector Berlioz, *Opéra Comique.* A disaster.
Wednesday, 12/30/46: *Robert Bruce,* Gioacchino Rossini, *Salle rue Le Peletier.* A triumph.
Wednesday, 1/13/47: Ball at *Le Château, Carnaval des Riches.*
Monday, 1/18/47: Ball at Mme. de Villars.
Tuesday, 1/19/47: Ball at the Belgian Embassy.
Wednesday, 1/20/47: Reception at the Duc de Nemours.
Tuesday, 1/26/47: Ball at la Princesse Pozzo di Borgo.
Monday, 2/1/47: Ball at Mme. de Béhague.
Tuesday, 2/2/47: Ball at Mme. de Lauriston.
Wednesday, 2/3/47: Death of Marie Duplessis.
Wednesday, 2/3/47: Ball at *la Salle Herz,* for the indigent English.
Thursday, 2/4/47: Ball at *l'Hotel Lambert,* for the indigent Poles.
Friday, 2/5/47: Burial at Montmartre, 24th division, 12th row, no. 46.
Friday, 2/5/47: Ball *rue de la Victoire,* Lady Normanby, Strauss.
Saturday, 2/6/47: *Grand Bal de l'Opéra.*
Sunday, 2/7/47: *Grand Bal de l'Opéra Comique.*

Sunday, 2/14/47: Ball at Frédéric Soulié's.

Tuesday, 2/16/47: *Mardi Gras.* Reburial, 15th division, 4th row, no. 12, close to Alfred de Vigny.

Saturday, 2/20/47: First night of *La Reine Margot,* AD 1, *Théâtre Historique.*

Wednesday, 2/24/47: sale of her belongings. "Paris is corrupted to the marrow" Charles Dickens, *Anglice.*

Monday, 2/2/52: First night of *La Dame aux Camélias,* AD 2, *Théâtre du Vaudeville.* A triumph.


## SECTION: LA TRAVIATA (7): CHANGING GRAVES


"I looked at her with love, nearly with terror,
thinking of what I was about to suffer for her —

                              foreknowing it."

Singing out of desperation
the end of romantic tradition,
my own course changing in the middle of the poem
because I no longer believe in love the way I had believed
                    it to inform our breathing:

                    Perrégaux transferring the grave
(married in Kensington, from Brompton Row, *Anglice,* 2/21/46
no. 106, folio 53, vol. i, The Book of Marriages)
        making her countess:

            D2 opening the grave with his double:
the eyes two dropped pits, the lips gone over the teeth
bared like ape-fangs; the hair
that had run like a river *de tenebris,*
taut on green hollows / a stench from the whole compost,
            "The eyes! did you see the eyes?!"
he cried in his cerebral storm — that was to cure him
in fifteen days' coma "from the moral illness."

                    II

What is desperate is that we can't ensnare
the fullness of the word she spoke in its own moment,
that generosity fades, attention peaks and falls
so that there is nothing left of her we had thought,

128

literally, to live for,
but reputation. And that is the crop of the *oeuvre:*
the romantic *marasmus:* fevers, obsessions, rages,
anything to delay love that has gone to seed,
a hunger satiated, a thirst quenched, the passage
of her delineations into a model of the soul —
so that the beloved at last is emptied, drained,
and, her womanhood lost, bows out in her despair,
         diminished beyond blood. . .


"Her affections broken, time after time / obeisance
to the needs of passing entanglements / jumping from love
to love, after love, after love — not knowing, alas,
why she choked off so quickly a nascent tenderness,
         a dawn of hope,
she had become indifferent to everything,
        paying no more attention
to love today than to tomorrow's passion."

### III

"She had lived the life a little, Sir, if you'll pardon the saying.
Now the poor lady's dead, and her remains
as heavy or as light as an honorable woman's.
        There were complaints about her in this row.
I told them, I did, fat, twice-a-year bankers
trailing their own flowers, and see what flowers!
carving tears on tombs they've never wept!
Believe me if you will, Sir, I never knew this lady:
nevertheless, I love her, the poor child, I take good care of her,
and let her have camellias at the market price.
        She is my favorite dead.
We, Sir, must love the dead: we are so busy with them
we scarcely have the time to love anything else."


Marie, you are older now.
You have survived up to twenty-eight, and I am no longer D2.
I am about as old as D1, when he nearly drave his son mad,
and as D2 when he had settled into *la belle morale.*
        Furthermore, you are not sick in any way,
though your analyst's bills put Marguerite's expenses in the shade.
I am supposed to entertain the arguments you used
so brilliantly to prove to D2 that he could not afford you —
though now it's a matter of status, profession, good sense
        rather than the madness of whores.

We have thirty-five days before your disappearance.
After which you will settle for the West Coast and a comfortable bore
who happens to be your thesis adviser.

Is it any wonder, then, that I half receive you
into my half-raised arms? In my Delaware garden
cancer at work
harries the rose crop.
There is half a rose,
perfectly opened in one half, the other cut away,
gone where the caterpillars mash dead petals,
the mud of your face ground in death.


## SECTION: LA TRAVIATA (8): LETTER TO A FRIEND ON MY LADY OF NOW

"New Hope, 5/14/73, Dear X,
My lady of now compares favorably with the average Amerikan beauty,
and her name is Helen. Had she been pointed out to Paris by Aphrodite,
as the exchange for Troy, she would have had no grounds for complaint.
My lady of now is more Amerikan than Pokahontas, more pertinent
to the culture of both coasts, ignoring all between:
but she is about to implement her education by seeing the Rokkies.

I met my lady of now in unlikely circumstances
in a village nearby whose name signifies ground for Hope.
She is divorcing, but, since nothing is simple, she has a lover
three thousand miles away from here who satisfies her partly.
She has just come back from a visit to him
and we have something like thirty-five days to spend together
before giving each other up, when she becomes again *La Traviata*.

'I looked at her with great love, even more with terror, thinking
of the great suffering I was about to enter on her account.'
On the evening of her return she told me in detail,
and with awesome perspicacity, the reasons we couldn't make it.
Six hours later, joy achieved, she told me that she loved me.
I recognized the old yearning for completion in my own feelings,
a sinking of the gut at the thought of her when she is not nearby,
and even when she is nearby, and so close to my eyes I am blinded.

My lady of now has a delightful physical presence. Especially
the region between waist and knees, of a silken fullness

130

the golden kine were made of in the sun's gardens.
A Danae of gold, herself the golden rain, her hair down there
honey and pepper, and the juices running from her: apricot.
Her breasts pear perfectly, though stretch-marked at the sides,
silver under the line of gold she measures her exposure by.
Her shoulders fill my hands and her armpits bury my nose
and her navel sweats with a promise of showers as we move to couple.

My lady of now is writing her thesis, and enjoys that compulsion
more than the pleasures of being in love. Aesthetic needs skeletal,
lowbrow in music, 'New Hope' in taste — and she treats her car
with the contempt of a goddess. When waking in the morning,
she is disturbed by birds rather than automobiles,
she is unmoved by nature and thinks my love of flowers ridiculous.
She tells me I will not wean her from her compulsions
when I try to explain that our freedom should be used and enjoyed.
I watch her relaxation in the night like a fanatic,
                    but she leaps from bed to library

at the first hint of daylight all the same. Thinking on Dumas
and his analysis of prostitution/adultery (—telling her his preface
should be translated for a feminist magazine), and thinking also
of S. and his graduate student C., whose compulsion with papers
is as great as Helen's with her thesis, I suppose to her an era
in which we men could be kept by our struggling intellectuals.
She says yes after all the years the female will has been held under.
If we are moving towards universal prostitution, as Dumas foretold,
then it would be nice if we men could relax a little now, I say,
but I am reminded we would have to cook the bacon and serve it
if the balance of provider and provided were to be upheld.

Yes, friend, these are problematic times. I have borrowed my Helen
from her future in Kalifornia at the foreskin of the Amerikan earth.
I try hard to remember whatever it is that I have learned of romance
in the belief that, under her compulsions, my Helen remembers also.
We have had our compulsions in our own day, and now take second place.
When she says she entered recently the technological age of masturba-
tion, or suggests vaseline for an experiment,
I harden still, with the blood of hope, and an obscure commitment
to the eros of our twentieth century.
                    And I bell her sweet tits to my eyes,
thinking our children will forgive us this one last trespass

before their making is taken out of our hands altogether. Best, etc."

## SECTION: LA TRAVIATA (9): TO OUR NORTHERN COUSINS

*From:* Pocahontas, of the Powhatan, in the place Jamestown, *Anglice:*
*To:* Asticou, Sagamore of Kenduskeag, Abnaki-Penobscot, Somes Sound —

    "Out of Chesapeake Bay
our father Argall, Samuel: August 27, 1610:
'came to an anchor in nine fathoms in a very great Bay'
    Hudson, Henry, a year before (un-named)
calling it, after De La Warr, Peer of England —
glossing over / the places I remind you,
standing between us and our Northern Cousins:
    Bay of New Amsterdam,
    Long Island Sound,
    Vineyard / Nantucket,
    Cape Cod Bay,
    Massachusetts Bay,
    Gloucester (pater noster C.O. ), peer maritime,
    Casco Bay — Booth Bay, all *Anglice*

Takes Brunswick (Stowe House, birth of Uncle Tom),
Takes Bath, *encyclopédie maritime,*
Takes Wiscasset and Edgecomb (N.D., friend to pater C.O.
    His canoe capsized, sea history),
Takes, in sea storm, in Tempest:
          MONHEGAN ISLAND
whale-back of Maine,
        out from Mañana, shearwaters, petrels,
in Smutty Nose, an ocean of rugosas, the whole town perfumed,
        bed of trailing yew among grasses,
rich botanical carpet,
        Lobster Cove, Christmas Cove, Gull Rock,
the *explosion fixe* over Washerwoman,
        pines sheathed in mist along Burnthead,
Cathedral woods, pine, spruce and fern,
        buzzsaw of warblers in the sighing trees,
Seal Ledges: eider tribes and bobbing young,
        Nigh Duck and Dead Man's Cove, our dead at sea,
and the deep horn in the night for our losing world:

Takes Camden
> wraps E.St.V.M. in her own clouds,
> takes her out and her moan once and for all,
> with all bad verse, all sodden craft & mediocrity,

Takes MONT DESERT:

> *Samuel de Champlain, père de la Nouvelle France.*
> *Henri IV, roi de France et de Navarre — — au Sieur des Monts*
> *seize cents quatre: le don de la Cadie.*
> French claim to "The Place": Philly (lat. 40°) — Montreal (lat. 46°).
>> September 6th, 1604
>
> *Le sommet de la plupart d'icelles*
>
>> *est desgarny d'arbres*
>
> *parceque ce ne sont que roches.*
>> *Je l'ay nommée:*
>> *L'ISLE DES MONTS DESERTS.*
> Blown by Argall for Jamestown (ship *Treasurer,* 1613).
>> English and French sharing the Isle thereafter.

II

My Lord —

A whole bevy of French women will descend upon your Summer capital
of Pemetic.
Item: Antoinette de Pons, Marquise de Guercheville,
(all-America grant, 1613.)
Item: Madame de Cadillac (Laumet-La Mothe, Dame de Douaquet
et des Monts Déserts, by patent, 1688).
Item: Madame Barthelmy de Grégoire, grand-daughter, 1786.
Item: Madame Bacler de Laval, 1792: Franco-American Cultural Center,
Taunton Bay.
> To the tune of *Vexilla Regis,* also:
Charles Maurice de Talleyrand- Périgord, sometime Bishop of Autun,
later Prince de Bénévent, Napoleon's right hand.
Le Vicomte de Noailles, 1796, (with Alexander Baring),
> 'Plagued by the immensity of Musketoes.'
Coin so scarce on the island, pins were used for small change,
> 'even for prostitution.'

My Lord —
In 1847, with the major immigration of Irish and English,
a ghost wife of AD2, one Marie Duplessis,
> sails in the mind of one N.T. for Norumbega."

In a Bar Harbor shell shop
framed portraits of the Ladies of Empire.
Among them all:
friend Mlle. Georges, mistress under N.1.
Ladies' Toilet Keeper, Palais de l'Industrie,
under N.3.
*Sic transit:* $35.00, with frame.
Marie is not among them.

*Elle est venue de France,*
*dans mon souvenir d'enfance, les parcs blancs comme l'écume.*
Takes Otter Point, with warblers. Storms.
Puffin turns out to be sea-skunk, off Gott & Black.
Takes Northeast Harbor: Benton (E.P.), at 50c. plus tax.
Takes Southwest Harbor, for the Cranberries: no sailing today.
Takes Bass Harbor, for Swann: no sailing today.
Book room of the Wendell Seavys': occultist lobstermasters.
The island shrunk like a nut in a frozen satchel.

Over Mount Desert campground
huge trees in wind,
illusion of a human body, gliding
above our faces:
end of the song, *l'estraviée* again —
Those French, those English,
the childhood language, split in the mind,
where shall I find my half, my missing half,
twin of my inner brain —
taking it out                    northwards. . .


## SECTION: LA TRAVIATA (10): ADDIO ROMANTICA


On a day like this (humidity obscene)
would have said to Colombo, Cristoforo,
(while humming Giuseppe nevertheless):
*eh! . . . . . . . alora! . . . . . . . . la Beatrice?*
this land UNINHABITABLE
go back / forget it / cut it out     of *anima mundi*,
(remember seeing, in Messina Bay,
six-five, the year of Early Bird,
"Leonardo da Vinci," *e* "Raffaello,"
Australia bound — other alternatives. . .)

Back into heat
off the Maine breeze,
thighs of New Hampshire and Green Mount,
6000 circuits, teleglobal system
        the heart confessed, *urbi et orbi,*
six gigacycles transmission, four reception,
        *on fait de la passion,*
twenty three thousand miles above equator,
        "conceived by swallowing a pearl"
one eye above one third of earth—


        Holding North
America the choice,
        the choice incarnate / no other place to go,
but she has been in place two hundred years at least
                and her singers, in place,
though I move with the fathers again, in re-enactment,
        take *mon Etat du Maine, querida Santa Fe*
in fee against the English and the Dutch,
              her other poets have been IN PLACE:
        and I their infant?


      "I made a garden on top of the rocky isle of Monhegan
      in May that grew so well
      it served for sallets in June/ July." John Smith, 1614, Englishman.

*La deux, la Canadienne*
down from their North, back to the coast of Me.,
brushing the wind off my car,
        Ontario: a multitude,
        *La Belle Province:* some less,
        Prince Edward Island: one taxi cab,
while I pass the presidential mountains,
        the green cascades of fern
in the thighs of Vermont
        holding to earth, and North, and beyond woman (as I mistake it)


Through Plainfield-Grossinger,
in sight of Mont Réal,
equivocal charm of frontiers,
through elegant Woodstock,
Hassidic summer places,
Bennington's lovelies,
back towards Pa. in muggy heat, monsoon,

to the raped body of Nouvel Espoir,
warped furniture, mice in the files,
                    and spider's sweat,

Singing Giuseppe still, his Violetta,
            not one magnifico paid for her portrait
to leave her smile behind in elegy —
            seven drawers in her night-table,
one lover to each day of the week (de Villemessant),
            siren of souls: not one / not back alive (Gautier),
and *"Dame aux Camélias, mystère de notre époque,"*
            conceived by swallowing a pearl. . .
Her habits pall upon him like a shroud,
            O Europe, weary catacomb of so much hope!

    *"Il est difficile de ne pas voir ce que cherche le XIXème:*
    *UNE SOIF CROISSANTE D'EMOTIONS FORTES*
    *est son vrai caractère."* Stendhal, 1817, Frenchman.

Walking all night, insomniac,
head in a huge kashmir (red),
her body lost in the tent of a white gown
            ("the Holy Land to the Promised Land"),
burned all her letters except thirty (Romain Vienne):
            those lost in San Francisco earthquake
when Sarah Bernhardt brought *La Dame* to Atlantis
            — check dates and details —
sombre / elegiac / attachments (e.g. Franz Liszt)
            lost without trace in the biography:

She goes, la Romantica, from dead eye-level,
    she goes, la Gnostica, from between Scylla and Charybdis,
she rises, la Esoterica, from the Sinai peak —
    she is taken with cold in her bones,
            with his poems in her eye-sockets, decomposed, running,
                shredded by mice in files,
                slimed by spiderfeet in boxes,
                decomposed by fungus at the edges of flesh,
she has passed into his soul so completely
    that mortal woman is diminished beyond blood.

| 6 vols. | Rabelais |
|---|---|
| 1 vol. | Cervantes |
| 1 vol. | Prévost |
| 1 vol. | Molière |
| 2 vols. | La Fontaine |
| 5 vols. | Marivaux |
| 2 vols. | Rousseau |
| 1 vol. | Goethe |
| 7 vols. | Chateaubriand |
| 9 vols. | Byron |
| 11 vols. | Hugo |
| 4 vols. | Sue |
| 3 vols. | Lamartine |
| 28 vols.+ | Alexandre Dumas, Père |
| 3 vols. | Vigny |
| 11 vols. | Thiers |
| 8 vols. | Scott |
| 1 vol. | Musset |
| ? vols. | Pound |
| ? vols. | Stevens |
| ? vols. | Williams |
| ? vols. | Rexroth |
| ? vols. | Patchen |
| ? vols. | Olson |
| ? vols. | Duncan |
| ? vols. | Mac Low |
| 1 vol. | New American Poetry. |

"*Et puis, pour en finir avec toutes ces histoires,*
to escape this pain, to avoid it for ever,
*para matar a la muerte una vez en fin*". . . Nathaniel Tarn, 1973,
American.


And he chose between two sightings, for lack of time:
old covered bridges, built like barns: *Labor's Cathedrals* –
the solid "Lovejoy," the "Sunday" 's elegance –
rather than bare white breast above the hill
    talking to sky
in whole earth-language, computer to computer,
    thou. fifty words per minute,
    Atlantic system (Andover, Maine)
                EARTH STATION INTELSAT

*AND SHE PASSES ONCE MORE,*
                    *SPREAD-EAGLED OVER EARTH,*
            her voice a whisper from white space,
            while the bridges span our lives into Atlantis
                            and the mountains sit it out

and North: Ontario
            and North: Quebec,
            The Maritimes,
            and North: My Newfoundland, my Labrador!

            and flat pole at the top, in soar of snow,
            white skullcap of the dream, or still or scudding,
            Antarctic template from the South's sole root
                            and the mountains sit it out:

                                    and North. . .


## SECTION: LA TRAVIATA (11): THE LAST ILLUSION


            (When I had parted from her, who held me seven years)

to the land at the other end of the wind,
lovely island through the world's age
shaped like a whale in the wine-blue ocean,
beyond the sunken precinct where philosophers had ruled,
the singing shrine where no sorrows reign,
where the roses are like weeds in the streets of town,
where no punishing wind, no snow, and never rain
foil tools at work in fields, while men bask under trees,
and corn's self-sowing and self-harvested

            (not tenderness for sons, duty to age,
            nor love I owed to wife that should have gladdened her)

to the land whose rivers may well have led to Eden,
the first sin skirted on the shoals,
which is nothing but the name the past gives to the future,
the first, or apple, sin: *o felix culpa!*
the second sin of corn: *o felix culpa secunda!*
sailing for wisdom with compass and canvas
beyond the borders of the inhabited world

138

to a place where there is a denudation of people,
where the birds talk like scholars in many languages

      (my men being slow and old when we came to that gate
      chose to deny the world in the sun's track
      and with our stern turned towards morning. . .)

but the island was peopled with playful children
believing paper spoke and asking beads from the sky,
begging for colors from the sky in trade for corn,
that were too cheap in the salons of turquoise —
and we were those who had come from under the world
to take their own world from them.
*Quicquid praeter Africam, et Europam est, Asia est:*
Was *this* Cathay? — these were not wise enough to be souled. . .

And it came to me in a dream, when I was grappled by them,
that I was brought before a splendor of feathers
and ordered to lay my head down on a stone,
but the child came from beside him and took my head in her arms
asking my life. Whereat, she was given it,
and I made a son to the King. Being later told
this was a simile of entrance into kingship, no genuine danger —
but took it out a little on my reading public

and also that the land at the other end of the wind
was full of nubile beauties who sang and danced for men,
after which they took us into their house
and everyone wanted me, crying "Love me, love me,"
so that it seemed I could not have endured so many loves /
but this was not prostitution as it turned out,
nor even free love, nor the beginning of commune,
but merely the offering of a companion, for a luxury at night.

II

      She had argued that she would give up her wealth and follow
me that was now the one man on earth she could abide. As she
said this, her black hair glistened as if moist with mist, or
it could have been tears from her native sky. She con-
fessed she had been born on the great island at the end of the
world, and that it was time she returned there in any event
to savior the natives. For she had adopted an orphan child
by mail the month before. She spoke of her youth as half a

horse, when she raced the clouds in the southern deserts, and of her battling with waves as tall as towers under the spruces of her birthright. Whence from half snake, she had gone to fish, and finally bird, in other realms of North and West. She possessed the land, *dueña* thereof. And was ready to purchase many acres more, on our two accounts.

But had not reckoned with the languor
that had crept into her bones in the ancient world
where she had sat for years oblivious to the people
in blaze of music. She had become addicted
to the culture of the terminal empires, denying
and neglecting the simple crafts of her own yard.
It was opera for her every night, fine meals,
camellias every morning, and pearls,
it was the company of fine gentlemen, who, more or less discreetly,
kept her in the style to which she had become accustomed.

And when she had attempted to turn towards what she had thought was "home," maps and charts had powdered in her hands — and had we followed her directions, we would have lost ship and crew both in great batter of rock. When the oldest woman of Europe landed on her native shore, many dusky maidens came to her crying, and holding her shoulders, whose names were Pocahontas, and Malitzin, and Tekakwitha, and Sacajawea, and Jacataqua, lamenting: "Now that thou art come, Maria Colomba, daughter of doves, must we lie down and be reduced to dust?" But she undressed herself of her crinolines, and appeared in the perfection of her own darkness, and ordered them that they should denude themselves likewise, and follow her in the dance. Whereupon the scenario was enacted as aforesaid — but here, I enjoyed them all one after another. . . Only, when I awoke in the morning, it was as if fallen from a great height, from an ocean cliff, and there was not one companion of them all to bind my wounds and comfort.

### III

And I am become as a land of ghosts

as a tree full of bird-song but no birds

where the mist clings to branches like cotton

and the wind sings mourning

140

From the other side, it was as if we had been calling for this, as if the weight of our need was such that it had magnetized the seas, and called a great pole to ourselves up from the place where the sun sets, and which we had named: the western gate,

and had placed all our dreams there, in who knows what hands. . .

and as if all the singers had assembled on the shores of the old land, standing before the flattened doors and tables at the edge of the cliffs that had seemed to be made as springboards for the great passage, and with but a short elegy for those they were to leave behind — who had lost the sense of hearing — they all, with a common accord in history, leapt into the westering sea, and were carried by fish or whale or albatross to the furthest edges of the ocean. . .

there, with darker women than themselves, to make new races. . .

but, having carried choice gifts to the King of the land, who, though he did not at first condescend to like them, became at last so enamored of possessions that he turned all the energies of his people to their fabrication, and made slaves of them until they also wanted nothing but these goods, and, at last, the whole land having been delivered into the hands of those whose chief business it was to make, advertise, barter and sell these goods, at whatever price, at whatever sacrifice and whatever beastliness in the reduction of men to animals of burden, who were no longer THE PEOPLE:

so that the ghosts at last, even they, had lost their tongues. . .

then it seemed indeed that we HAD come from under the world

to take their own world from them. . .

IV

The last woman of the old dispensation has gone back to her dust.
And the first woman of the new world is going back to her dust.
She keeps on changing the color of her hair, as in a movie,
she becomes a blonde on the way to Kalifornia, West of the West,
she is an androgyne going out into Space, which is West of Kalifornia,
lugubrious in the night of spiders, they all leave for distant lots.

And when the people of this continent have made their shopping list:
the oil of the other people of the world and their labor,
the blood of the other people of the world and their labor,
the flesh of the other people of the world and their labor,
they then fall to buying health and happiness and parity freedoms,
then they think of purchasing a second automobile and a frigidaire
and three sets of air-conditioning devices and a radio-clock-t.v.

and all that done, they come to the places they have baptized
with all the variants of the word *Hope,* which means hope for bargains:
Hope-Well, and Hope-Truly, and New Hope, and Good, Clean, Used-Hope,
              and, leaving behind any reality whatsoever,
          they buy the shoddy, the useless, the ugly and the bad
in the name of the singers of liberty who left our world so long ago.
At night, when everyone is drunk, they piss on the trees of the town,
and they shit in the streets, and they masturbate in the parking lots,

and then they bugger the injun princess in the municipal square

where they had left her only some years back

                              as she bounced out of the forest:


                    *infin che'l mar fu sovra noi richiuso. . .*

142

# A POSTFACE: THE DICTATION

*for G. & S.Q.*

*Voices beginning a dictation.*
    *Evil perchance is some greater good*
*so great it has become invisible.*
    *Voices of books in silence with their leaves all read.*
    *I have looked for the city / inside the ocean*
*inside the tear of one eye / many years / painfully    (and)*
    *it is true I have been as a child inside a man's coat.*
    *The walls with voices and no perjury.*
    *Great Fathers in their halls of light, their colleges,*
*space-height above the house.*
    *What have they said (she ((within him)) ), what have they asked?*
*This is* nel mezzo */ do you know how long* nel mezzo *IS?*
    *the height of one man who cannot stand his life.*
    *Him I shall know, and she (within him) speaking.*
*Sd. the angel of mind: you are in exile from your name*
    *as from a land: you who are all in exile. . .*
*(my brother called me "thief" — but can you steal an angel?)*
    *(and): Speak to him through her, as you would in yr. own name.*
*Sd. the angel of love: you have exhausted woman,*
*the "eros" is weary, you may turn to the balance of matters now.   (and)*
    *She opens pages, singing libretti of the dead.*
*And the angel of strength: my father is a small man, he fears,*
    *timidly he waits for his death, fearing his superstitions.*
    *I see him in this cold and cannot move him.*
       *While the angel of healing healed.*
    *O at my back the arms turning to feathers and the white*
               *river of his hands!*

            \*\*\*

            *One said: your life*
*is the life of my husband: the places you have traveled are*
*his places, his silences yours, return is yours in these his colonies.*
            *She added: it is cold*
*in my entrances and my departures. Deep in bed it is frigid.*
*Neither of you has been able to warm me into anything like love.*
            *She stood*
*among her ages, caught in the photographs: 1909,   1920,   now.*
            *Another said:*
*I am your mother before your birth, you might have loved me.*
*She gave me a name willingly.*

And one was beautiful
before her time and, achieving her youth, no longer was shining.
I loved them both.

He spoke of angels
of the moment you faint in
unable to bear yr. own life,
he was also the voice on the phone:
"I am going mad and no one can help me!"
One cd. not tell him he loved hself. too much.

He spoke about angels assuming the face of my name and my terms
of exile. She suckled my father in a black rain of hair.

\*\*\*

I shall call this a "prelude," remembering other "preludes" where
angels inform men that they encompass them.
Speak the truth to her, life, that you cannot lie about more than
you wd. lie, of death, to yr. life (and)
My heart is of feathers / scales, I bear the god of war in my heart
when weary with the smallness of discretion.
But, love, that I bear in my hands, when my hands are doing the
work they were created to perform, then only:
and this is the sense of angels, moving about the sky's tides
with great and sure rapidity. (CATAR/ACT). Cataract cataract cataract.
All of us: philosopher-lovers, all of us above the random thought, the
perdition of energy, the fall — the loss, the loss, the loss,
O lovely numbers of her heart when she resembles us!

\*\*\*

I remember my life
how it was sweet in the early days though I didn't know it then.
Of this STAR
the matter of this, stuff of, texture,
of this grand jury of our birth-day,
with his single eye, a laser among calendars,
OF THIS, STAR, the moment of joy is the,
when with a single hand we clap aloud
and, look, brother,
when it was about to fall and galvanize
the rigid earth to action, when it was,
about to live through all the times of death
each one of us can mangle / then. . .it. . .SANG, can you HEAR IT???

144

The, woman, stupid, with, impotence.
Do , you , think , it , is , only , males , who , are , impotent?
Beware, you who think that impotence is only male.
But, in her stupidity, she also was part of, also,
the, pattern of holding, her, arms, held, and, blessed.

***

Sharp as the knife ' mong grasses
                    sharp as a scent of leaves, coming, to come,
                         this primavera d'
amore, which is yet to come     (and)
                    ya iba por las flores, with her bosom
                         white among garlands:
for to tell / truth / her elbows
                    thrust to her hands and fingertips the leaves
                         she cd. not open
                    through singing. Wife of Hades is her name
but we should not: say, in unclassic days,
                    no we shd. not
                    say that, though we still (open!)
ah, and shall always as we name our task. . .

***

Brother Rabbi who gave rise to this poem / and Brother Rabbi who
gave it voices, tell me I can go to the stone and find tears inside
when it splits, and tell me I can bathe in the tears and caress the
small river fish, and tell me there is grey spawn in the river bed / the
black and white of mourning. . . . . .and tell me. . . . . .where the roads
go. . . . . .when you rise up early. . . . . .and feel no requirement of
sleep.
Shall be an energy of heart. Shall be again, an energy of beginning.
Shall be an energy of homing as bird, hiding as animal – among the
shadows. Yes, and shall be, a flight of sparrows to this Ark – the
common kind – like men in mud: no doves, no ravens.

          Go forth now and lie down to sleep
          and place yourself at the disposition of
          whatever shines above you like the sun.
          Shd. there be no presence, no radiance there,
          send yrself out of yrself a little while,
          flowing out from fingertips to toes, and,
          it shall be as a mirror before you, but greater,
          standing tall beyond the ceiling of the room
          and conversing with you /// face to face.

We shd. take pity of ourselves on the flood
and take care of ourselves among the wreckage.
These debris that you see around you:
they are the words of our silence.
I was going to say they were the words
of our poems, but something opened in the wings
of sleep and I was unable to tell you that.

Of the Ark, I shall tell you only that it is made of the timbers of
our voices. Of Ark, there is no need to say more than one word:

RELEASE.

\*\*\*

I was looking for a moment
when, instead of saying,
this happiness would be too great
(it has never happened this way, you know
nothing can live up to the expectation),
happiness wd. suddenly seem effortless,
flowing of itself by its own right
and the good tidings would come in with the light
and I wd. see her face at the door
when I expected to see it.

For that because, he had been here a while below / and sang his
moment
willingly, and with a courage took it on, as far as it wd. go:
for that because:
he was willing to try continually and be worthy of salvacioun,

no doom was written on his page, his page was blank in heaven,
and they awaited him there with all the alternatives he'd wished,
desired through darkness, all that he could do.

Voices fading naturally, with his wishing to sleep.
Like a second nature you might almost say.
No requirement of sleep, you understand.
Bees humming when it's Summer.

\*\*\*

The night was radiant beyond telling but I tell you now.
Radiant the night, graced with her radiant name.
Radiance as a tide of light moving out

*from where she stood against the radiant walls.*
*Where she stood in her anguish, her radiant arms held high,*
*since nothing she could do escaped the radiance.*
*He had been brought into the radiance by the puppet master,*
*the master of lodestones and mines,*
*asking whether he could do anything to be of service to him.*
*He admitted that he could not honor the master of the radiant house*
*for dwelling in a creature of his & being unable to take away his eyes.*
*When all was done (i.e. the radiant chanting, the radiant dancing,*
*and the radiant rocking backwards and forwards, and radiant praising),*
*there was the radiance of a calm evening in which they stood finally*
*together. Then it became difficult not to melt into her side,*
*that side of her radiance which his life was touching.*
*There was a radiance of sobs inside her, returning to her home,*
*and inside him: several breaks with the present*
*and a committal to her house of hair, that he should live inside it.*
*For the radiance, it was a matter of her transparent skin*
*and a religiosity in the eyes which signed her of his house.*
*He went round for a while afterwards, within the radiance,*
*kissing the tops of strangers' heads, and their hands,*
*as he had done in his many priesthoods, and she followed,*
*(though kissing the puppet master was not easy, however hard they tried)*
*from time to time escaping back into one of her radiances,*
*one he could not see too well, being blind round corners,*
*but came back and followed truly and they ended together among sleep.*

    *Blessed art thou, of radiant presences the center*
    *that maketh the diamond to shine forth from the coal*
    *and the moment to leap forth from the aeon!*

*Everything is redeemed said one in my sleep, whose name and title*
*I did not catch*
                          *upon the introduction.*

147

It is only just to mention that, during the writing of these poems, the following texts were part of the author's mental climate. He has sometimes followed the familiar practice of treating another author's words as "found poetry." The list is, of course, far from complete.

Philip Barbour: *Pocahontas and Her World*
Lewis Richard Farnell: *The Cults of the Greek City States*
Joseph Gaer: *The Legend of the Wandering Jew*
Robert Graves: *The Greek Myths*
Johannès Gros: *Une Courtisane Romantique*
Claude Lévi-Strauss: *La Pensée Sauvage*
Samuel Eliot Morison: *The Story of Mount Desert Island*
Raphael Patai: *The Hebrew Goddess*
Raphael Patai & Robert Graves: *Hebrew Myths*
Bernadino de Sahagun: *The Florentine Codex (*Anderson & Dibble eds.*)*
Gershom Scholem: *Major Trends in Jewish Mysticism*
Zwi Werblowski: *Joseph Karo, Lawyer and Mystic*
Edgar Wind: *Pagan Mysteries of the Renaissance*